The Two Sources of Indian Asceticism

Johannes Bronkhorst

The Two Sources of Indian Asceticism

MOTILAL BANARSIDASS PUBLISHERS
PRIVATE LIMITED • DELHI

First Indian Edition: 1998

Die Deutsche Bibliothek — CIP-Einheitsaufnahme

Bronkhorst, Johannes:
The Two sources of Indian asceticism/Johannes Bronkhorst -
Bern; Berlin; Frankfurt a. M.; New York Paris, Wien: Lang 1993
(Schweizer asiatische Studien: Monographien; Vol. 13)
NE: Schweizer asiatische Studien/Monographien

ISBN: 81-208-1551-3

Cover illustration:
Ascetic practices of the Bodhisattva, Museum, Lahore

Also available at:
MOTILAL BANARSIDASS
41 U.A. Bungalow Road, Jawahar Nagar, Delhi 110 007
8, Mahalaxmi Chamber, Warden Road, Mumbai 400 026
120 Royapettah High Road, Mylapore, Chennai 600 004
Sanas Plaza, Subhash Nagar, Pune 411 002
16 St. Mark's Road, Bangalore 560 001
8 Camac Street, Calcutta 700 017
Ashok Rajpath, Patna 800 004
Chowk, Varanasi 221 001

PRINTED IN INDIA
BY JAINENDRA PRAKASH JAIN AT SHRI JAINENDRA PRESS,
A-45 NARAINA, PHASE I, NEW DELHI 110 028
AND PUBLISHED BY NARENDRA PRAKASH JAIN FOR
MOTILAL BANARSIDASS PUBLISHERS PRIVATE LIMITED,
BUNGALOW ROAD, DELHI 110 007

Table of contents

Preface

This book promises, in its title, to deal with the two sources of Indian asceticism. This is· somewhat misleading. For direct information about these sources does not appear to be available. The oldest literary remains of India, primarily the *R̥gveda*, do not contain unambiguous information about the object of our interest, and nor does the archaeological evidence. Speculations can be based on them, but no certain, or very probable conclusions.

The somewhat younger literature – though perhaps already far removed from the sources concerned – is far more interesting in this respect. It shows a clear awareness on the part of its authors that there were two different kinds, or currents, of asceticism. It also shows the tendency of these two currents to unite, and to become ever more indistinguishable as time goes by. It therefore allows us to conclude that they were distinct from the beginning. In other words, the two currents have, or rather had, two different sources.

This much seems clear, and certain. More precise information about the sources themselves is hard to come by. As said above, the early Vedic texts and the archaeological evidence do not help us much. The present study therefore largely ignores them.

There is another word in the title that requires elucidation. It is *asceticism*. This word is here used in a rather general sense: it covers the whole range of physical and mental exercises from extreme mortification to certain forms of 'gentle' meditation, it being understood that all these forms of asceticism constitute the whole, or at least a major part, of the life of the ascetics concerned.

The preparation of this volume has taken several years, during which I have had the opportunity to discuss its contents with various colleagues. I thank all those whose comments have enabled me to further clarify different points. Most of all I thank Prof. Gerald J. LARSON, who went through the final draft, and made a number of helpful suggestions.

Preface to the second edition

This edition is largely identical to the first one, published by Peter Lang, Bern, in 1993. The occasion has however been grasped to correct minor errors, mainly typographical, in the main text. Only the Introduction has been rearranged to some extent. Some observations – dealing with new publications or publications that have belatedly come to my attention – have been added to the footnotes. These publications have themselves been added to the bibliography. New footnotes can be recognized by the use of an asterisk (*). Additions to existing footnotes are indicated as such. For ease of comparison, the page numbers of the first edition are indicated in the margin.

Introduction [3]

The origin of Indian asceticism has puzzled investigators. The reason is clear. Asceticism plays a central role in classical Hinduism and in the two other religions that arose on Indian soil, Buddhism and Jainism. Yet the earliest surviving documents of India, the Vedas, breathe a different atmosphere. No quest for liberation from this and the next life, no withdrawal from the world, but rather a wish to obtain all the goods this life has to offer: life until an advanced age, sons, cows, riches, etc.

In spite of this, early researchers believed that the Vedic tradition inspired the non-Vedic manifestations of the ascetic spirit. JACOBI (1884: xxii f.), for example, concluded from the similarities that exist between the main vows and obligations of the Jaina and Buddhist monks on the one hand, and certain rules for ascetics in the law-books of Gautama and Baudhāyana on the other, "that neither the Buddhists nor the Jainas have in this regard any claim to originality, but that both have only adopted the five vows of the Brahmanic ascetics" (p. xxiii). Similar remarks had been made before him by BÜHLER (e.g., 1879: 193 n. 13) and MÜLLER (1879: 318), and were to be made by KERN (1896: 73) afterwards. Ideas current at the time about the antiquity of the Vedic age no doubt facilitated this conclusion.[1] The question of how asceticism fitted into Vedic religion remained, however, unanswered. It is primarily J.W. HAUER's
(1922) merit to have initiated a search for antecedents of later [4]
Yoga in the Vedic texts, and thus to have tried to bridge the chasm that appeared to exist between Vedic religion and the later ascetic movements.

Meanwhile T.W. RHYS DAVIDS (1899: 215 f.), P. DEUSSEN

1. Cf. OLIVELLE, 1974a: 11; BRONKHORST, 1989.

(1906: 17f.; German original 1899) and especially R. GARBE (1903) had proposed a different origin for the religious current that manifests itself in the Upaniṣads and in Buddhism and Jainism.[2] This current, GARBE maintained, is no continuation of or development out of Vedic religion, but rather a reaction against it.[3] This reaction originated with the Kṣatriyas, members of the warrior caste, who thus expressed their discontent with the ritualism of the Brahmins.[4]

GARBE's proposition remained within the confines of Vedic society. The discovery of urban centres belonging to the pre-Vedic Indus civilisation, on the other hand, focused attention on the non-Vedic elements in Indian culture. Sir John MARSHALL (1931: I: 52) described a figurine on a seal from Mohenjo-daro as a "God, ... seated ... in a typical attitude of Yoga",[5] and a
[5] statue as "seemingly in the pose of a yogī, and it is for this reason that the eyelids are more than half closed and the eyes looking downward to the tip of the nose" (id., p. 44, cf. p. 54).

2. See already MÜLLER, 1879: 306.
3. So also LÉVI, 1898: 11.
4. A reflexion of this point of view is still to be found in WILTSHIRE, 1990: xvi: "The Buddhist and Jain traditions had their origin in the Śramaṇa Movement which began as a protest by Kṣatriyas against the Brahmanic stranglehold on religion and society." (cp. also p. 227 f.) See also FRAUWALLNER, 1953: 47-48; JAINI, 1970: 43. SCHNEIDER (1989: 56 f.) distinguishes between Kṣatriya-religion and Brahmin-religion, but assigns the *ātman*-doctrine squarely to the latter. BAKKER (1989: 48-49 n. 64) thinks, in view of the fact that both Kṣatriyas and Brahmins play an equal role in these texts, that Upaniṣadic philosophy is mainly a joint product that has developed outside the traditional orthodox Vedic schools.
5. This interpretation has been criticized in SRINIVASAN, 1984; During CASPERS, 1985: 234 f. BASHAM (1989: 5) calls the evidence for Yoga in the civilization of the Indus "so tenuous that the suggestions [that Yoga was practised] are quite unacceptable except as faint possibilities". (Added in the 2nd edition:) A renewed evaluation of this issue will have to take into considerations some of the elements added to the discussion by Thomas MCEVILLEY (1981).

Indian asceticism, then, might have an altogether non-Vedic origin. This is indeed the position taken by several authors, some of whom speak of a Śramaṇa movement outside the Vedic pale, which however influenced Vedic religion.[6]

A fair number of scholars these days emphasize nonetheless the continuity that exists between the Vedic sacrificial tradition on the one hand, and the penchant towards asceticism on the other. Consider, for example, J.C.HEESTERMAN's article "Brahmin, ritual, and renouncer", first published in 1964, and reprinted in 1985 in *The Inner Conflict of Tradition* (pp. 2-644). HEESTERMAN finds in the Vedic ritual a development toward ever decreasing involvement with others. The pre-classical sacrifice, HEESTERMAN claims, involved rivalry between different parties. This 'agonistic cooperation' has disappeared in the classical sacrifice, where only one institutor of the sacrifice (*yajamāna*) remains. This *yajamāna*, however, is still dependent, this time upon his officiants. The next step, therefore, would be [6]
in the direction of discarding the officiants. In HEESTERMAN's words (1985: 38-39): "The development of brahmanical theory, set off by the individualization of the ritual, did not stop at the point where the host-guest, protagonist-antagonist complemen-

6. See, e.g., DUTT, 1924: 60 f.; LAMOTTE, 1958: 6 f.; PANDE, 1974: 321 f.; WARDER, 1980: 33 f. Lilian SILBURN (1955: 135 f.) combines the last two points of view and ascribes a role to both Śramaṇas and Kṣatriyas. HARVEY (1990: 10-11) presents another melange: "Brahmins learnt of yogic techniques ... from ascetics whose traditions may have gone back to the Indus Valley Civilization. Such techniques were found to be useful as spiritual preparations for performing the sacrifice. Some Brahmins then retired to the forest ... Out of the teachings of the more orthodox of these forest dwellers were composed the Upaniṣads ... The ideas expressed in the Upaniṣads ... were being hotly debated, both by Brahmins and wandering philosophers known as *Samaṇa*'s, who ... rejected the Vedic tradition ..." OLIVELLE (1992: 21) believes "that when the evidence is examined completely it does point to a profound conflict between [renunciation and Vedic religion], a conflict that cannot be adequately explained if renunciation was in fact 'an orthogenetic development of Vedic thought'".

tarity was fused into the single unit of *yajamāna* and officiants. It had to advance to its logical conclusion, that is, the interiorization of the ritual, which makes the officiants' services superfluous". With the interiorization of the ritual, HEESTERMAN thinks, "we touch the principle of world renunciation, the emergence of which has been of crucial importance in the development of Indian thinking".

One might of course raise doubts as to whether historical developments have to follow such rigid rules.[7] It is however clear that elements of asceticism accompany the Vedic ritual. This is also the opinion of Hans-Peter SCHMIDT (1968), who follows HEESTERMAN in believing that "[t]here are ... in the Vedic ritual some significant details to be found which can be regarded as precursors of the later *vānaprastha* and *parivrājaka*" (p. 651). His own article draws attention to the fact that "the whole ritual is pervaded by acts meant for immediately eliminating any killing and injury – the acts of appeasing (*śānti*)" (p. 646). It is even possible to speak of 'a ritual *ahiṃsā*-theory' (p. 649). This ritual *ahiṃsā*-theory, SCHMIDT suggests (p. 649-650), "is the ultimate source of the later renunciatory *ahiṃsā*-doctrine".

Again it is possible to raise doubts. One might recall, with DONIGER and SMITH (1991: xxxii n. 39), that "[w]hile it is true that in Vedic ritualism there was expression of concern that the
[7] sacrificial victim should not suffer or cry out ..., that he accepts his fate voluntarily and eagerly and so forth, all this is part and parcel of sacrificial ideologies everywhere". HALBFASS (1991a: 113), too, questions SCHMIDT's conclusions: "Was there really a 'ritual *ahiṃsā*-theory'? And in what sense can we say that this 'ritual *ahiṃsā*-theory is the ultimate source of the later renunciatory *ahiṃsā*-doctrine'? Does it not seem more likely that external factors contributed to these developments which sub-

7. This is probably also OLIVELLE's (1992: 70) intention when he states that "Heesterman's theory depends too heavily on the development of ideas".

sequently led to a sharp antagonism between Vedic ritualism and *ahiṃsā* as two basically different forms of religious orientation?"

A different approach is taken by Joachim Friedrich SPROCKHOFF in a number of publications, most notably in his article "Die Alten im alten Indien" (1979). SPROCKHOFF, too, thinks that the Vedic ritual is one of the foundations of *saṃnyāsa* (1987: 256). But he recognizes another root in the situation of the aged individual. Briefly stated, *saṃnyāsa* is here presented as the decision of the aged father to leave all his possessions to his sons and to disappear from his house and village.[8] Such decisions, originally no doubt taken under pressure (if they were not cases of downright eviction), took on religious dimensions and resulted in the prescription that, ideally, the aged twice-born should end his days as solitary wanderer. The stage of *vānaprastha* should then be considered a first step in this direction.

It will be clear that both the approaches outlined above face [8]
serious difficulties. If we accept that asceticism is originally a non-Vedic phenomenon, we will be hard put to explain the ascetic features which seem to be inseparable from the Vedic sacrifice. If, on the other hand, we postulate a Vedic origin, it is hard to explain the coherence of ideas encountered in the non-Vedic manifestations of asceticism. Also certain chronological
questions – such as the beginnings of Jainism, reputedly 250 [9]
years before Mahāvīra – are then hard to answer.

There is a third possibility. Indian asceticism might have two sources, the one Vedic, the other non-Vedic.* This possibility

8. Already in 1879 Heinrich ZIMMER (1879: 327-28) had drawn attention to the possibility in Vedic India to banish ("aussetzen") the aged father; see also HABERLANDT, 1885.

* TSUCHIDA has argued in a recent publication (1997) that there may further have been a kṣatriya tradition of asceticism. Further research will be required to substantiate this.

avoids the problems connected with the two earlier ones. Moreover, it agrees with the textual evidence, as this book will show.**

This 'two sources' solution is, to be sure, not completely unknown to the secondary literature. Jean VARENNE (1971: 12), for example, observed: "L'accueil du Yoga par le brahmanisme ... est dû ... surtout au fait que les rituels védiques connaissaient des pratiques analogues à celles que prône le Yoga ..." Walter O. KAELBER (1989: 110) suggests "that the brahmacārin's career is in large measure a forerunner *and* legitimizing model for the initially heterodox practices of ascetics later assimilated into orthodoxy as forest hermit (*vānaprastha*) and world renouncer (*sannyāsin, bhikṣu, pravrajita, parivrājaka, muni, yati*)". Mircea

** OLIVELLE (1995: 13-14) comments in the following manner upon the first edition of this book: "I remain unconvinced by both sides of [Bronkhorst's] argument, not because they do not contain some elements of truth, but because all by and large ignore the social and economic factors that underlie the emergence of these new religious forms ..." Here OLIVELLE has obviously missed my point. Social and economic factors may explain what we find in our texts, and should certainly not be ignored. But before we look for explanations, we have to know what needs to be explained, and for that we depend on the texts. This book deals with the textual evidence.

OLIVELLE then continues: "That the Indian society in the Gangetic valley was composed of diverse ethnic groups, many of which were of non-Aryan origin, is obvious. It is equally obvious that the religious beliefs and practices of these groups must have influenced the dominant Aryan classes. It is quite a different matter, however, to attempt to isolate non-Aryan traits at a period a millennium or more removed from the initial Aryan migration." This may be correct, but does not constitute a criticism of the thesis defended in this book, which makes no claims as to the Aryan or non-Aryan origins of the beliefs and practices dealt with.

OLIVELLE concludes: "The most we can say is that the ascetic traditions contain beliefs and practices not contained in the early vedic literature, and that they are in many ways opposed to the central vedic ideas." This is quite correct, and it turns out that two currents of asceticism can be distinguished (and are distinguished in the texts), one of which deviates considerably more from the "central vedic idea" than the other. This is what the present book is about.

ELIADE (1969) finds precedents of Yoga in both Brahmanism and 'aboriginal India'. Steven COLLINS (1982: 31) observes that "the phenomenon of world-renunciation in India seems also to have drawn on extra-Brahmanical roots". Albrecht WEZLER (1978: 111 n. 304) draws attention to the "Tatsache, dass es, gleichgültig, of die weltflüchtige Askese nun nur **eine** Wurzel hat, nämlich brahmanisch-ritualistischer Herkunft ist oder nicht, zahlreiche und verschiedene Formen der Weltentsagung gegeben hat, die zugleich eine deutliche Abkehr vom Brahmanismus und traditionellen Ritualismus darstellten"; he is of the opinion that this whole complex of questions needs further investigation and rethinking.

The 'linear' approach which induced most scholars to look for one source of Indian asceticism, induced them also to look upon different forms of asceticism as being 'earlier' and 'later',
even in cases where both occur in the same text, or in the same [10]
story. An interesting example are the studies of HACKER (1978), WEZLER (1979) and SHEE (1986: 1-30), all of them dealing with the *Mahābhārata* story of Śamīka and Śṛṅgin.[9] Only SHEE (1986: 7) has pointed out that the two forms of asceticism described in this story cannot necessarily be ordered linearly into an older and a younger one.

Phenomena of the same type – such as asceticism in ancient India – may, but do not necessarily all belong to the same current of development. Indeed, the present study intends to show that the different forms of asceticism that can be distinguished in India belong to (at least) two different currents. These currents did not fail to influence each other in subsequent times, and become ever more difficult to distinguish from each other as time goes by. But they are clearly distinguishable in the early texts.

9. See also chapter 11, below.

[It will become clear in the following pages that one of the two currents to be considered has close connections with the belief in transmigration, each new birth being in accordance with one's actions. An earlier study (1986) has drawn attention to the
[8] complex of ideas that links this belief to the different forms of asceticism meant to put an end to those rebirths. Briefly stated, these forms of asceticism aim at the elimination of all actions. They do so, grosso modo, in two ways. One of these is to literally abstain from all, or most, activity. This leads to a number of ascetic practices which share the common theme of motionlessness of body and mind. The other way centres around the insight that the body – and the mind – do not constitute the true self. This second way encouraged the development of different 'philosophies', which specified how body and self are related to each other; all these philosophies share the belief that the self does not participate in any action.

This complex of ideas constitutes an organic whole.[10] It is therefore not without risk to isolate one aspect or another from this complex and 'trace' its history back to the Vedic texts. The fact that Vedic religion knows the phenomenon of renunciation (*saṃnyāsa*), or non-violence (*ahiṃsā*), does not necessarily prove that therefore this complex of ideas derives from Vedic religion.]***

10. This is not to deny that "[i]n its concrete totality, the doctrine of *karma* and *saṃsāra* is a very complex phenomenon, both historically and systematically" (HALBFASS, 1991a: 295).

*** This passage occurred, in slightly different form, on pp. 7-8 of the first edition. Klaus BUTZENBERGER has adopted in a recent publication (1996) a line of reasoning which he describes as a kind of *methodological positivism*, and which implies that "If all specific features and characteristics of [the doctrine of the transmigration of souls] prove to be derivable from Indian texts, we confess to be in no need of assuming major or even relevant influences from other sources ... *Non enim entia sunt miltiplicanda praeter necessitatem.*" (p. 58). BUTZENBERGER furthermore claims on the same page "that the extant Indian texts are perfectly sufficient in order to trace the sources, motives and origins of [that doctrine]". He then presents a scheme of how ideas about the afterlife might, or should, have developed. The inherent weaknesses of such schemes have already been pointed out while discussing HEESTERMAN's ideas, above. BUTZENBERGER's approach is also limited by the fact that he merely seeks to exclude "pre-Aryan" and "extra-Indian" influences, overlooking the fact that, just as Vedic religion and thought underwent major changes in the thousand years or so following its appearance in India, also the religious world views of those Indian who were less directly, or not at all, connected with Vedic religion might have undergone major changes. Most seriously, however, BUTZENBERGER does not consider the fact that the Indian tradition itself clearly distinguishes between different currents of practices and beliefs, as documented in the present book.

Part I

The *āśrama*s

Chapter 1. The *Āpastamba Dharmasūtra* [11]

Patrick OLIVELLE, following earlier authors,[1] observed in 1974 that a number of old Dharmasūtras – the oldest, by common consent – present the four *āśramas* not as four stages in the life of a high-caste Hindu, but as four alternatives, four options regarding how to spend one's life after an initial period in the family of a teacher. It would not be correct to take this to mean *that* these Dharmasūtras allow one to skip one or more intervening *āśramas*; the very idea of succession is absent. The importance of this observation has gone largely unnoticed. It implies that one may become an ascetic without ever having been a householder, and therefore without ever having obtained the right to sacrifice. This, of course, is difficult to explain for those who believe that early Indian asceticism arose from the sacrificial tradition.

The first and most important text to be considered is the *Āpastamba Dharmasūtra* (ĀpDhS).[2] This text deals with *brahmacārins*, *parivrājas*, *vānaprasthas* and *gṛhasthas*, in this order. This remarkable sequence – which deviates from the later
temporal sequence *brahmacārin, gṛhastha, vānaprastha, pari-* [12]
vrāja (or *saṃnyāsin*) – is explained by the fact, already referred to, that no chronological sequence in the life of an individual is intended.

Note to begin with that the ĀpDhS prefers the choice of *gṛhastha* to the three other ones, and even rejects the other ways

1. DEUSSEN, 1909: 128-29; FARQUHAR, 1920: 40; WINTERNITZ, 1926: 218-19; KANGLE, 1986: III: 151. See further BROCKINGTON, 1981: 92; OLIVELLE, 1984: 100; SPROCKHOFF, 1991a: 15.
2. Cf. SPROCKHOFF, 1991a, which also mentions variant readings in the parallel passages in the *Hiraṇyakeśi Dharmasūtra* and in the *Satyāṣāḍha Śrautasūtra*.

of life in which, according to the ĀpDhS, the Vedic injunctions are not obeyed (2.9.23.10); we shall see that the way of life of the *parivrāja* is explicitly stated to be against the scriptures (2.9.21.15). Yet the text presents a clear and interesting description of these ways of life.

Sūtras 2.9.21.7-16 deal with the *parivrāja*. We learn that the wandering ascetic is chaste (8), without (sacrificial) fire, without house, without shelter, without protection, he is a *muni* who utters words only during recitation, who obtains support of life in a village, moving about without interest in this world or in the next (10);[3] he uses only relinquished clothes (11) or, according to some, no clothes at all (12); he leaves behind truth and falsehood, pleasure and pain, the Vedas, this world and the next, searching his self (13).

In this enumeration no painful mortifications are included. The life of the *parivrāja* is no doubt simple, extremely simple, but the only remaining thing that interests him is not the capacity to endure hardship, but rather to find his self.

This is extremely interesting. It shows that the *parivrāja* of the ĀpDhS is engaged in one of the two ways of escape from the never ending cycle of birth and rebirth determined by one's
[13] actions, briefly explained in the Introduction, above. This belief is not unknown to the ĀpDhS. Sūtra 1.2.5.5, for example, states that "some become Ṛṣis on account of their knowledge of the scriptures (*śrutarṣi*) in a new birth, due to a residue of the fruits of their [former] actions".[4] Recall that this way of escape may imply that, once the true nature of the self has been realized, the aim has been reached. The remainder of the description of the wandering ascetic confirms that this possible implication was

3. SPROCKHOFF (1991a: 10 + n. 42) translates "für den es weder ein Hier noch ein Dort gibt". He further suggests (p. 17-18) that sūtra 10 was originally metrical and read: *anagnir aniketaḥ syād aśarmāśaraṇo muniḥ / svādhyāya utsṛjed vācaṃ grāme prāṇadhṛtiṃ caret //*.

4. ĀpDhS 1.2.5.5: *śrutarṣayas tu bhavanti kecit karmaphalaśeṣeṇa punaḥsaṃbhave; yathā śvetaketuḥ*.

known to the author of the ĀpDhS. Sūtra 2.9.21.14 states: "In an enlightened one there is obtainment of peace" (*buddhe kṣemaprāpaṇam*). The next two sūtras then turn against the preceding description. Sūtra 15 begins: "That is opposed to the scriptures" (*tac chāstrair vipratiṣiddham*). No. 16 continues: "If there were obtainment of peace in an enlightened person, he would not experience pain even in this world" (*buddhe cet kṣemaprāpaṇam ihaiva na duḥkham upalabheta*). These sūtras confirm again that the wandering ascetic is concerned with liberation through enlightenment; they also show that the author of the ĀpDhS rejects this as impossible.

Here it must be pointed out that the ĀpDhS contains another section – to be precise: the eighth Paṭala of the first Praśna – which appears to be in contradiction with the above rejection of the *parivrāja*. That other section sings the praise of what it calls 'the obtainment of the self'. Indeed, "there is no higher [aim] than the obtainment of the self" (1.8.22.2). A number of ślokas are then quoted, possibly from a no longer existing Upaniṣad,[5] which elaborate this theme (1.8.22.4 – 23.3). This section does
not concern only the *parivrāja*. Its concluding lines (1.8.23.6) [14]
enumerate the virtues that have to be cultivated in *all* the *āśramas*, and which, presumably, bring about identification with the universal soul.[6] The puzzling bit is the quoted stanza

5. NAKAMURA (1983: 308 f.) points at the similarities with the *Kāṭhaka Upaniṣad*.

6. The concluding portion is obscure: ... *iti sarvāśramāṇāṃ samayapadāni tāny anutiṣṭhan vidhinā sārvagāmī bhavati* "these (good qualities) have been settled by the agreement (of the wise) for all (the four) orders; he who, according to the precepts of the sacred law, practises these, enters the universal soul" (BÜHLER, 1879: 78); "these are [the virtues] which must necessarily be observed thoughout all of the [four] stages of life. He who puts them into practice according to the rules becomes one who goes everywhere" (NAKAMURA, 1983: 308); "these (virtues) have been agreed upon for all the āśramas; attending to them according to the rules one becomes possessed of that one who is going everywhere (= one becomes united with the universal Self)" (SCHMIDT, 1968: 641). The

1.8.23.3, which seems to say that the aim of the religious life (*kṣema*) is reached in this life: "But the destruction of faults results from the yoga here in this existence. Having eliminated [the faults] which destroy the creatures, the learned one arrives at peace (*kṣema*)."[7] It appears, therefore, that the author of this portion of the ĀpDhS accepts what is rejected as impossible in the discussion of the *parivrāja*. Do we have to conclude that the ĀpDhS had more than one author?][8]

We turn to the next question: The ĀpDhS deals explicitly
with the way of insight, practised by the *parivrāja*. Does this
mean that it knows the alternative way of inaction? Yes it does,
[15] and it speaks about it in connection with the forest-dweller
(*vānaprastha*). The forest-dweller, like the wandering ascetic, is
chaste (19), without (sacrificial) fire,[9] without house, without
shelter, without protection, he is a *muni* who utters words only
during recitation (21); until this point the description is identical

---

commentator Śaṅkara believes that one of the quoted stanzas refers to a state of renunciation (*sarvasaṃnyāsa*), see NAKAMURA, 1983: 307 and 318 n. 10. This interpretation is in no way compelling. The relevant portion of the stanza (1.8.22.8) reads: (*yaḥ*) ... *prādhvaṃ cāsya sadācaret.* This means no more than: "and who acts always in accordance with its path". No far-reaching conclusions can be drawn from this.

7. ĀpDhS 1.8.23.3: *doṣāṇāṃ tu vinirghāto yogamūla iha jīvite / nirhṛtya bhūtadāhīyān kṣemaṃ gacchati paṇḍitaḥ //* Tr. NAKAMURA, 1983: 308. Note the use of 'yoga' here and in 1.8.23.5.
8. The question is also raised in GAMPERT, 1939: 8.
9. The edition reads *ekāgnir*; this must be a later 'correction' of original *anagnir*, which occurs in the otherwise identical sūtra no. 10 (beginning). The presence of a sacrificial fire is in any case excluded by the absence of house, shelter and protection. (According to sūtra 2.9.22.21 (*agnyarthaṃ śaraṇam*) a shelter is required for a fire.) See also SKURZAK, 1948: 17 n.1; and SPROCKHOFF, 1979: 416; 1991a: 19f.

with the one of the wandering ascetic.[10] The forest-dweller, unlike the wandering ascetic, wears clothes made from products of the jungle (2.9.22.1), he supports his life with roots, fruits, leaves and grass (2); in the end only things that come by chance support him (3); subsequently he depends successively on water, air, and ether alone (4).[11] It is clear that the forest-dweller reduces progressively his intake of outside matter. Eating is reduced, then stopped, only water being taken in. Subsequently this too stops, while breathing remains. Then this too comes to an end, expressed by the words that the forest-dweller now depends on ether alone. It is not necessary to recall the fasts to death of Jaina and other ascetics in order to show that the author of the ĀpDhS was also acquainted with what might be called the 'way of inaction'.

The part of the ĀpDhS so far considered, then, teaches the four *āśrama*s as four alternative ways to lead one's life. The same alternatives are enumerated at ChU 2.23.1, be it that different terms are used. The passage reads, in translation: [16]

> There are three divisions of Dharma. The first is sacrifice, study [of the Veda] and munificence. The second is asceticism and nothing else (*tapa eva*). The third is the *brahmacārin* who lives in the family of a teacher (and who causes his self to sink in the family of the teacher).[12] All of these obtain an auspicious world. [But] he who resides in brahman goes to immortality.[13]

10. The term *muni* is used in connection both with the *parivrāja* and with the *vānaprastha*. A similar general use of *muni* is found in the epic (SHEE, 1986: 175).
11. ĀpDhS 2.9.22.1-5: *tasyāraṇyam ācchādanaṃ vihitam / tato mūlaiḥ phalaiḥ parṇais tṛṇair iti vartayaṃś caret / antataḥ pravṛttāni / tato 'po vāyum ākāśam ity abhiniśrayet / teṣām uttara uttaraḥ saṃyogaḥ phalato viśiṣṭaḥ /*
12. BÖHTLINGK (1889: 99) considers this a gloss.
13. ChU 2.23.1: *trayo dharmaskandhāḥ / yajño 'dhyayanaṃ dānam iti prathamaḥ / tapa eva dvitīyaḥ / brahmacāry ācāryakulavāsī tṛtīyo ('tyantam ātmānam ācāryakule vasādayan) / sarva ete puṇyalokā bhavanti / brahmasaṃstho 'mṛtatvam eti //*

The preference of the *Chāndogya Upaniṣad* is the exact opposite of that of the *Āpastamba Dharmasūtra*. But the four possible ways of spending one's life are the same for both. We can take this passage from the ChU as a confirmation that we have so far correctly understood the ĀpDhS. Let us return to the latter text.

The only connection with the Veda of the *parivrāja* and of the *vānaprastha* as described so far in the ĀpDhS, is their recitation of Vedic mantras (*svādhyāya*; so sūtras 2.9.21.10 and 21). These ascetics have nothing to do with Vedic rites, neither in their real, external form, nor in an interiorized form. Our text, in any case, does not say a word about it. Or rather, it confirms that these ascetics cannot perform Vedic sacrifices, by now introducing another type of forest-dweller, one who does sacrifice, and who for this purpose must take a wife and kindle the sacred fires. This other type of forest-dweller is described in sūtras that represent the opinion of 'some' (*eke*), which may
[17] indicate that this description derives from a different source altogether. This other forest-dweller finishes his study of the Veda, takes a wife, kindles the sacrificial fires and performs the rites prescribed in the Veda (2.9.22.7); he builds a house outside the village, where he lives with his wife and children, and with his sacrificial fires (8).[14] This alternative way of life of the forest-dweller is also characterized by an increasing number of mortifications (sūtras 2.9.22.9 – 23.2). Sūtras 2.9.23.7-8 are especially interesting: they show that this kind of forest-dweller obtains supernatural powers: "Now they accomplish also their wishes merely by conceiving them; for instance, (the desire to procure) rain, to bestow children, second-sight, to move quick as

14. It is the succession described in these two and the following sūtras that is announced by the word *ānupūrvya* in sūtra 6, not "the successive performance (of the acts prescribed for the *āśramas*)". OLIVELLE (1984: 101) may therefore be mistaken in thinking that these rules constitute "an exception to the rule that an *āśrama* has to be selected immediately after completing one's Vedic studies". See further SPROCKHOFF, 1991a: 25, 27.

thought, and other (desires) of this description" (tr. BÜHLER, 1879: 158).[15]

It will be clear that the ĀpDhS describes, under the two headings of forest-dweller and wandering ascetic, not two, but three different forms of religious practice: 1) the way of insight into the true nature of the self; 2) the way of inaction, in this case: of fasting to death; and 3) a half sacrificial – half ascetic way of life.[16] Only one of these three ways of life has any connection with Vedic ritual. Yet the ĀpDhS is an orthodox Brahmanical text. It is hard to believe that its author, had he been aware of a connection between the other two ways of life and the Vedic sacrificial tradition, would have kept silent about [18] it. The conclusion seems justified that for him the way of life of the *parivrāja* and that of the *vānaprastha* – i.e., the one who does not sacrifice – stood quite apart from the Vedic rites. Being an orthodox Brahmin, it is not surprising that he preferred the life of the householder to its three alternatives.

We shall henceforth distinguish between 'non-Vedic' and 'Vedic' asceticism. We shall further assume that the two forms of asceticism described in the ĀpDhS that have no link with the Vedic sacrifice, are reflections in a Brahmanical text of originally 'non-Vedic' ways of asceticism. Besides these, the ĀpDhS describes one type of 'Vedic' ascetic. The practices of the Vedic ascetics are linked to the Vedic sacrifice; this is not true in the case of the non-Vedic ascetic. Indeed, the latter may not know the Vedic sacrifice from direct experience, and not infrequently he may not be entitled to, nor ever have been entitled to perform them. Vedic ritualism does not appear to play any role whatsoever in his ascetic endeavours. On the contrary, his efforts are directed toward liberation from rebirth, an aim which he may not share with his Vedic colleagues. The

15. ĀpDhS 2.9.23.7-8: *athāpi saṃkalpasiddhayo bhavanti / yathā varṣaṃ prajādānaṃ dūre darśanaṃ manojavatā yac cānyad evaṃ yuktam /*

16. SKURZAK (1948) had already drawn attention to the threefold classification of ascetics in the ĀpDhS.

aims of the Vedic ascetics are harder to pin down on the basis of the ĀpDhS. It may however be very significant that this text mentions the obtainment of supernatural powers in the context of the Vedic *vānaprastha*.

Consider now the three types of ascetics which Megasthenes distinguishes in Schwanbeck's fragment 41 (tr. MCCRINDLE, 1877: 98-102):

> Megasthenês makes a ... division of the philosophers, saying that they
> [19] are of two kinds – one of which he calls the Brachmanes, and the other the Sarmanes.
>
> The Brachmanes ... have their abode in a grove in front of the city within a moderate-sized enclosure. They live in a simple style, and lie on beds of rushes or (deer) skins. They abstain from animal food and sexual pleasures, ... Death is with them a very frequent subject of discourse. They regard this life as, so to speak, the time when the child within the womb becomes mature, and death as a birth into a real and happy life for the votaries of philosophy. On this account they undergo much discipline as a preparation for death. ... on many points their opinions coincide with those of the Greeks, for like them they say that the world had a beginning ...
>
> Of[17] the Sarmanes he tells us that those he held in most honour are called the Hylobioi. They live in the woods, where they subsist on leaves of trees and wild fruits, and wear garments made from the bark of trees. They abstain from sexual intercourse and from wine. ... Next in honour to the Hylobioi are the physicians, since they are engaged in the study of the nature of man. They are simple in their habits, but do not live in the fields. Their food consists of rice and barley-meal, which they can always get for the mere asking, or receive from those who entertain them as guests in their houses. ... This class and the other class practise fortitude, both by undergoing active toil, and by the endurance of pain, so that they remain for a whole day motionless in one fixed attitude.

One type of Brahmin ascetic is here described, besides two kinds of Śramaṇas. Megasthenes' remark about the embryonic nature
[20] of this life, and of death as a birth into another, better existence
is of particular interest. The Vedic texts look upon the conse-

17. The remaining portion is also translated in ZYSK, 1991: 28.

crated sacrificer (*dīkṣita*) as an embryo preparing to be reborn into another kind of existence.[18] It will also become clear in a later chapter that Vedic asceticism was in many respects a permanent form of *dīkṣā*.

Megasthenes' remarks about the two kinds of Śramaṇas are even more interesting, for they correspond almost exactly to the two kinds of non-Vedic ascetic of the ĀpDhS.[19] One of these stays in the forest, and survives on what he finds there. The other one begs for his food and, very significantly, is "engaged in the study of the nature of man"; we can safely interpret: this ascetic is in search of the true nature of the soul.[20] Both Śramaṇas are described as remaining motionless for long periods of time. This remark shows that these ascetics belong to the non-Vedic current.

Megasthenes' testimony constitutes a striking confirmation of the conclusions which we were able to draw from the ĀpDhS. Both sources state that there were two types of ascetics in ancient India, Vedic and non-Vedic. Both describe only one type of Vedic ascetic, and two kinds of non-Vedic ascetic. We cannot but believe that we are here confronted with fairly reliable descriptions of the actual situation, rather than with mere Brahmanic rationalizations.

Let us once more return to the ĀpDhS. This text uses the terms *vānaprastha* and *parivrāja*. *Vānaprastha* is used to denote [21]
both Vedic and non-Vedic ascetics; it is therefore difficult to

18. See, e.g., OLDENBERG, 1917: 405 f.
19. Megasthenes does not, therefore, refer to Buddhists; see also HALBFASS, 1991b: 207.
20. This kind of ascetic is further described as 'physician', and ZYSK (1990; 1991) has argued that Āyurveda in its origins is linked to non-Vedic asceticism. WOLZ-GOTTWALD's (1990) criticism of ZYSK's position overlooks the fact that the non-Vedic ascetics presuppose the existence of social milieus from which they recruited their members, and which most probably shared many of their ideas (such as the belief in rebirth, but also perhaps the 'empirico-rational' approach to disease).

determine whether this term belonged originally to the Vedic or to the non-Vedic realm. The term *parivrāja*, on the other hand, is here connected with non-Vedic ascetics only. This agrees with the use of the corresponding term *paribbājaka* in the Pāli Buddhist canon. Here it refers throughout to non-Vedic ascetics. No term corresponding to *vānaprastha* is found in these texts.[21] (The same is true of Pāṇini's grammar, which may have to be dated around 350 B.C.E. (HINÜBER, 1989: 34). The term *vānaprastha* is not mentioned, whereas *parivrājaka, bhikṣu, maskarin* and *śramaṇā* do occur. Patañjali's *Mahābhāṣya* (around 150 B.C.E.), on the other hand, mentions the *cātur-āśramya* under P. 5.1.124 vt. 1.)

The situation is different in the Jaina canon in Ardha-Māgadhī. Here the word *vānaprastha* (*vāṇa(p)pattha*) occurs a few times, always in connection with Brahmanical ascetics. We read here about *vānaprastha* ascetics (*vāṇapatthā tāvasā*), who are, among other things, *hottiyā,* which corresponds to Sanskrit *agnihotrikāḥ* according to the commentator.[22] According to one ms reading, these ascetics are also *sottiya,* which might correspond to Sanskrit *śrotriya*.[23] Interestingly, the Jain canon uses on some occasions also the term *parivrājaka* (AM *parivvāyaga/-ya*) to refer to Brahmins. The *parivrājaka* Khanda(g)a, for example, knows the four Vedas with their *aṅgas* and *upāṅgas*, and many other Brahmanical and *parivrājaka* texts (Viy 2.1.12). Essentially the same description is
[22] repeated for the *parivrājaka* Moggala (or Poggala) (Viy 11.12.16) and for the Brahmins Gobahula and Bahula (Viy 15.16, 36).[24]

21. See ch. 10, below.
22. Viy 11.9.6; Uvav 74; Pupph 3.4. Cf. DELEU, 1966: 122-23; 1970: 175; LALWANI, 1985: 184; JAIN, 1984: 300; LEUMANN, 1883: 163 s.v. *hottiya.*
23. See Viy 11.9.6 p. 517 n. 3.
24. See further JAIN, 1984: 302 f.

Chapter 2. *Saṃnyāsa* [23]

The ĀpDhS does not use the word *saṃnyāsa* or its cognates (*saṃnyāsin, saṃnyasta,* etc.). And indeed, it would be a mistake to associate these words with any of the ascetics so far described. The early texts use these terms in connection with an altogether different kind of ascetic. Very interestingly, these texts are not Dharmasūtras, but Saṃnyāsa Upaniṣads and a Śrauta Sūtra.

The ascetic dealt with in these texts has a clear link with the Vedic sacrifice. But unlike the Vedic ascetic considered above, this one interiorizes the sacrifice, and continues in this new way his ritual obligations. We first look at a short passage from the *Mānava Śrautasūtra* (MŚS 8.25) which deals with him.[1] This passage contains the term *saṃnyāsa*, but does not as much as mention the terms *vānaprastha* and *parivrāja*, or any of their usual synonyms. The rule of renunciation here described implies that the renouncer parts with all his possessions, and abandons the sacrificial fires. The text makes clear that one has to be a householder with children, and therefore married, in order to qualify for renunciation; this requirement does not surprise in the Vedic sacrificial context of the MŚS. More problematic is, at first sight, the abandonment of the sacrificial fires. In reality the renouncer does not abandon his fires, he rather makes them rise [24]
up within himself (8.25.6: ... *ātmany agnīn samāropayet*). Moreover, he heats himself at the three sacrificial fires (8.25.7: ... *āhavanīye gārhapatye dakṣiṇāgnau cātmānaṃ pratāpayet*); we may conclude, with SPROCKHOFF (1987: 241), that the renouncer increases his *tapas* during this operation. Sūtra 10 adds that he takes ashes from the three fires, but the following sūtras are too corrupt to allow us to conclude with certainty what

1. This passage was recently studied by J.F. SPROCKHOFF (1987).

he does with them. Sūtras 12 and 13 specify that henceforth his meals and certain other activities are his oblations. Sūtra 15, finally, tells us how the renouncer ends his days. The presence of twice *vā* 'or' seems to indicate that three alternatives are offered: 1) entering the fire, the road of the hero (*agnipraveśanaṃ vīrādhvānam*); 2) non-eating (*anāśakam*); 3) the *āśrama* of the aged (*vṛddhāśramam*). It is true that entering the fire and the road of the hero are presented, in some later texts,[2] as alternatives. The preoccupation of the renouncer here described with the sacrificial fires, which he has absorbed in his body, permits us to take the present passage at its word: entering the fire is the preferred, but also most difficult method of killing oneself, and is therefore called 'road of the hero'.[3]

The main elements to be noted in the passage from the MŚS are:

1) *Saṃnyāsa* is not brought in connection with the four *āśramas*.

[25] 2) The renouncer parts with all his possessions, including specifically the Vedic fires, which are interiorized.

3) The renouncer is or has been married.

4) He may decide to kill himself in some well-defined way.

We find these same elements in the *Kaṭhaśruti*.[4] However, the position of the *saṃnyāsin* with regard to the sacred fires is here inconsistent: p. 38 l. 7 f. states that they are interiorized, p. 32 l. 1 f. speaks rather of a transfer of the vital breaths into the fires. SPROCKHOFF (1976: 73 n. 20; 1989: 143) concludes

2. *Jābāla Upaniṣad* p.68 l.2-4 has: *ayaṃ vidhiḥ pravrājinām: vīrādhvāne vānāśake vāpāṃ praveśe vāgnipraveśe vā mahāprasthāne vā*; similarly in *Paramahaṃsaparivrājaka Upaniṣad* p. 279 l. 13 - p. 280 l. 1. The *Kaṭhaśruti* (p. 39 l. 3-4), on the other hand, presents 'entering the fire' and 'the road of the hero' together in such a way that it is not possible to decide whether they refer to one or two methods.

3. Instances where sacrificer and victim are identical are, according to SCHEUER (1975: 78 f.), the epic characters of Ambā and Aśvatthāman. For traces of self-sacrifice by fire in the Veda, see FALK, 1986: 37 f.

4. See SPROCKHOFF, 1989: 147 + n. 2.

rightly that the *Kaṭhaśruti* text cannot be a unitary work. This does not change the fact that the *Kaṭhaśruti* contains a particularly clear passage showing that the *saṃnyāsin* is dead to the world:[5]

> Having made the sacrificial priests place all the sacrificial utensils on the limbs of the sacrificer (i.e., of his own), he should place (his five breaths, viz.) *prāṇa, apāna, vyāna, udāna* and *samāna,* that are in (the five sacrificial fires, viz.) *āhavanīya, gārhapatya, anvāhāryapacana, sabhya* and *āvasathya,* all [five of them], in all [of the five sacrificial fires].

The connection between this passage and Vedic descriptions of funeral rites is beyond doubt,[6] so much so that the only reason for believing that the present passage does not describe a real sacrifice – i.e., the burning alive of the renouncing sacrificer – is [26]
the following context, which describes how the renouncer cuts off his hair, throws away his sacrificial cord, regards for the last time his son (if he has one), and wanders off.

The initial prose portion of the (*Laghu-*) *Saṃnyāsa Upaniṣad* – to be separated from the following ślokas, and from most of what follows in the Upaniṣad – satisfies three of the above four points.[7] The person described is an Āhitāgni, and therefore presumably a married man.[8] We also read that two fires are interiorized (*dvāv agnī samāropayet*; p. 17 l. 8); according to SPROCKHOFF (1976: 63) these are the Gārhapatya and Āhavanīya fires. Very interesting is further the remark that the

5. *Kaṭhaśruti* p. 31 l. 7 – p. 32 l. 3: *yajamānasyāṅgān ṛtvijaḥ sarvaiḥ pātraiḥ samāropya yad āhavanīye gārhapatye 'nvāhāryapacane sabhyāvasathyayoś ca prāṇāpānavyānodānasamānān sarvān sarveṣu samāropayet.* Cf. SPROCKHOFF, 1989: 147-148; OLIVELLE, 1992: 129-130.
6. See SPROCKHOFF, 1989: 148 n. 11; BODEWITZ, 1973: 131 ff.
7. See SPROCKHOFF, 1976: 36 f., esp. 52 f.; 1991.
8. Some texts on Dharma allow for the possibility that someone kindle the sacred fire without marrying and becoming a householder; see chapter 3 below.

saṃnyāsin to be wishes to "go beyond the *āśrama*(s)" (*āśrama-pāraṃ gaccheyam*; p. 15 l. 3). This does not necessarily imply that the four *āśrama*s were known, for the person described, being an Āhitāgni, is probably a householder. Yet it justifies the conclusion: "Der Saṃnyāsa ist ausdrücklich *kein* Āśrama" (SPROCKHOFF, 1976: 54).

The relationship between *saṃnyāsa* and the *āśrama*s is further elucidated by a passage from the *Āruṇi Upaniṣad*. Here we read (p. 5 l. 3 f.) that a householder (*gṛhastha*) or a *brahma-cārin* or a *vānaprastha* can abandon his sacrificial cord (*upavīta*) and interiorize the fires (*lokāgnīn udarāgnau samāropayet*; p. 6 l. 1-2). There is no indication in the text that these three ways of life were thought of as succeeding each other; the order in which
[27] they are presented suggests the opposite.[9] The precise significance of the terms *brahmacārin* and *vānaprastha* in this context is not clear.[10] P. 6 l.3 speaks of a *kuṭīcara brahmacārin* who abandons his family; this is obviously not the same as a Vedic student who lives in the family of his teacher.[11] And if it is true that our passage speaks of interiorizing the Vedic fires (*lokāgnīn udarāgnau samāropayet* is somewhat obscure), also the *vāna-prastha* must be assumed to maintain a Vedic fire; this of course leads to no difficulty if a 'Vedic' *vānaprastha* is meant here.

9. This passage does not agree with p. 9 l. 1-2 which allows a boy to renounce already before the *upanayana*; the present passage speaks of abandoning the sacred thread, which is obtained at the *upanayana*. It is therefore hard to believe that the two passages were originally part of one and the same text.

10. See SPROCKHOFF, 1981: 59-60, which speaks – in connection with ChU 8.5 – about the wider sense of *brahmacarya*. See also *Arthaśāstra* 1.3.9-12 which, while enumerating the *āśrama*s as four alternatives, mentions *brahmacarya* as a duty of the *vānaprastha*; see ch. 3, below. Note further that the *Nyāyabhāṣya* on sūtra 3.1.4 (Ānandāśrama ed. p. 193) speaks of the practice of *brahmacarya* in order to reach liberation: *tatra muktyartho brahmacaryavāso na syāt*.

11. On *kuṭīcara*/*-caka*, see SPROCKHOFF, 1976: 128.

It will be clear from the above that some of the oldest texts that describe *saṃnyāsa* do not link this institution to the four *āśramas*, even though at least one of these texts knows the term *āśrama*, and another one the terms *gṛhastha*, *brahmacārin* and *vānaprastha*. The earliest texts that describe explicitly the four *āśramas*, on the other hand, do not mention *saṃnyāsa*.[12] To this opposition another one must be added: the ĀpDhS, as well as the texts to be considered in chapter 3 below, introduce the *āśramas* as alternatives; *saṃnyāsa,* on the other hand, is reserved for men of a certain age. We shall return to this important distinction.

One might try to explain these oppositions, pointing at the different kinds of texts which represent the opposing points of [28]
view: the *āśramas* are described in Dharmasūtras, *saṃnyāsa* primarily in Upaniṣads. The Dharmasūtras, one might argue, represent the interests and points of view of the *gṛhasthas*, while only the Upaniṣads were directly inspired by the ascetic ways of life.[13] However, this approach to the texts is not without serious risks. It provides an excuse for not taking seriously a large proportion of our sources about ancient Indian asceticism. Moreover, it decides a priori that the *saṃnyāsa* of the early Saṃnyāsa Upaniṣads and the ascetic *āśramas* of the early Dharmasūtras concern the same phenomenon. (And this a priori decision would then without much further difficulty entail that the whole of ancient Indian asceticism derives from Vedic antecedents.)

No such a priori position will here be taken. If *saṃnyāsa* and the two ascetic *āśramas* concern the same thing, the texts must provide evidence for this. Our inspection of the texts so far, however, suggests something quite different: the four *āśramas* in the earliest texts do not cover *saṃnyāsa*; and *saṃnyāsa* is no *āśrama*!

12. A partial exception is VasDhS 10.4, which reads in the context of the *parivrājaka*: *sannyaset sarvakarmāṇi vedam ekaṃ na sannyaset / vedasannyasanāc chūdras tasmād vedaṃ na sannyaset //*. See OLIVELLE, 1981: 269; 1984: 127 f.

13. This is essentially SPROCKHOFF's approach (1979: 376).

In a way this was to be expected. SPROCKHOFF (1976: 291 f.; 1979; 1980) has rightly drawn attention to the fact that the *saṃnyāsin*, though living in a biological sense, is dead to the world. Indeed, the ceremonies that introduce him into this final state of 'life' include his symbolic cremation, as we have seen. But clearly the four *āśrama*s, being presented as four alternative ways of living one's life, should not cover a way of 'living one's death'!

One thing, however, seems clear. The moment efforts were
[29] made to include *saṃnyāsa* into the *āśrama*s, a temporal ordering of those *āśrama*s became virtually inevitable. For *saṃnyāsa* concerned the aged. This too has been convincingly shown by SPROCKHOFF. A text like the (*Laghu-*) *Saṃnyāsa Upaniṣad,* for example, introduces *saṃnyāsa,* very significantly, as an alternative to death for those healthy *āhitāgni*s who have not yet died. In other words, it is the mutual adaptation of *āśrama*s and *saṃnyāsa* which introduced temporal order into the former.

A few words must finally be said about the number of *āśrama*s. The ĀpDhS enumerates four of them, but only three are Brahmanic in the proper sense. In fact, we have seen that of the two ascetic *āśrama*s only the *vānaprastha* can be Vedic, the *parivrāja* is completely non-Vedic. The addition of *saṃnyāsa* to the *āśrama*s in later times changed the situation, but at a price; for *saṃnyāsa* was originally no *āśrama*. In the light of these considerations it is not without interest to see that one verse of the *Manusmṛti* (2.230) speaks of 'the three *āśrama*s'; this in spite of the fact that elsewhere (6.87) this same text enumerates four *āśrama*s.[14] Also MBh 12.109.6 speaks of three *āśrama*s. MBh 12.311.27, finally, speaks of the three *āśrama*s that are based on the state of householder, and that do not please him who looks for liberation.[15]

14. Cf. SPROCKHOFF, 1991a: 39 f.

15. MBh 12.311.27: *na tv asya ramate buddhir āśrameṣu narādhipa / triṣu gārhasthyamūleṣu mokṣadharmānudarśinaḥ //*

Chapter 3. The four *āśrama*s as alternatives [30]

We shall now briefly consider some other early texts which present the four *āśrama*s as alternatives.

The rejection of all forms of withdrawal from the world which we found in the ĀpDhS we find again in the *Gautama Dharmasūtra* (GDhS). This text concludes a discussion of the four *āśrama*s with the words: "But the venerable teacher (prescribes) one order only, because the order of householders is explicitly prescribed (in the Vedas)" (3.36 (=1.4.35): *aikāśramyaṃ tv ācāryāḥ pratyakṣavidhānād gārhasthasya* ...; tr. BÜHLER, 1879: 196). That is to say, the author of this text accepts but one of the four *āśrama*s. This does not stop him from providing a short description – which represents the opinion of 'some' (3.1 = 1.3.1) – of the other three; the names used are *brahmacārin, bhikṣu* and *vaikhānasa* respectively. We are here of course especially interested in the *bhikṣu* and *vaikhānasa* (3.11-35 = 1.3.10-34).

The first thing to be noted is that neither of these two, *bhikṣu* and *vaikhānasa,* appears interested in finding the true nature of the self. Both engage rather in various forms of restraint and mortification. An important difference between them is constituted by the different ways in which they obtain their nourishment: the *bhikṣu* begs, and is for this reason allowed to enter a village, the *vaikhānasa* never enters a village and lives by what he finds in the forest.[1] An even more important
difference, at any rate from the point of view of our present [31]
investigation, concerns their position with regard to Vedic ritual. The text is silent about the *bhikṣu*'s link with it. The *vaikhānasa,*

1. The *vaikhānasa,* though never entering a village, is stated to live in a *vana* (3.26 = 1.3.25), not in the *araṇya*!

on the other hand, establishes a fire in accordance with the *Śrāvaṇaka* (v.l. *Śrāmaṇaka*; 3.27 = 1.3.26: *śrāvaṇakenāgnim ādhāya*), which is the authoritative book of the *vaikhānasa*s (*vaikhānasaṃ śāstram*) according to the commentator Haradatta.

We might here be tempted to identify this *vaikhānasa* with the 'Vedic' *vānaprastha* of the ĀpDhS. There is however a major difference. For the *vaikhānasa* is not necessarily married! In normal circumstances he would therefore not be entitled to kindle the Vedic fire. The solution which was apparently devised for ascetics bent on an ascetic life-style from a young age, consisted in some special rules for the *vaikhānasa*s, which allowed them to kindle the Vedic fire without first having to get married.

The GDhS gives us no details concerning these special rules of the *vaikhānasa*s. It is not impossible that they have found expression in the *Vaikhānasa Dharmasūtra* (VDhS), a text which, in its present form, seems to be younger than the GDhS.[2] VDhS 8.6 requires that a householder who plans to take his abode in the woods (*vanāśramaṃ yāsyan*), whether he be in the possession of a sacred fire (*āhitāgni*) or not, should churn a *Śrāmaṇaka* fire and take it with him to his new abode.

So the *vaikhānasa* of the GDhS appears to combine elements of the 'Vedic' and 'non-Vedic' *vānaprastha*s in the ĀpDhS: he is no longer required to marry, and is yet allowed to kindle the Vedic fire, so as to become a sacrificing ascetic. But the *bhikṣu* of the GDhS, too, is an amalgam of different elements. He
[32] corresponds to the *parivrāja* of the ĀpDhS, but without his most important characteristic, viz., the search for the self. He also corresponds to the *saṃnyāsin*, but is not stated to have interiorized his sacred fires. Indeed, the *bhikṣu* may never have kindled these fires to begin with.

Also the *Vasiṣṭha Dharmasūtra* (VasDhS) presents the four *āśrama*s as alternatives. The *vānaprastha* is here once again

2. CALAND, 1929: xvii – xviii.

described (adhy. 9) in terms which are often identical with the GDhS. Most importantly, he kindles the fire in accordance with the *Śrāmaṇaka,* and become in this way *āhitāgni* (9.10: *śrāmaṇakenāgnim ādhāyāhitāgniḥ syāt*). However, after six months he gives up fire and house, and dwells at the root of a tree (9.11: *vṛkṣamūlaniketana ūrdhvaṃ ṣaḍbhyo māsebhyo 'nagnir aniketaḥ*). The result of all this is that the *vānaprastha* goes to heaven, to infinity (9.12: ... *sa gacchet svargam ānantyam* ...).

Chapter 10 deals with the *parivrājaka*. This chapter contains a number of quoted verses, which show that the VasDhS derived its information regarding this ascetic form from another source. We learn from these verses that the *parivrājaka* abandons[3] all (sacrificial?) actions (10.4), that his mind is concentrated on his self (*adhyātmacintāgatamānasa*), that he will certainly not return (10.17), that he aims at liberation (*mokṣa*; 10.20, 23).

It seems clear that the *parivrājaka* of the VasDhS remains close to the *parivrāja* of the ĀpDhS. Both pursue clearly non-Vedic ideals, viz., liberation to be obtained through knowledge of the self. The fact that interiorizing the Vedic fire is not mentioned is not surprising: the way of the *parivrājaka* has really [33]
nothing to do with Vedic ritual, and the text has made no effort to impose such a link. True, the *parivrājaka* is enjoined not to abandon one Veda, that is, to recite mantras (10.4) or, even better, the syllable *oṃ* (10.5); but this does not affect our conclusion. After all, we are dealing with an orthodox Vedic text, which cannot but show a tendency to vedicize non-Vedic practices.

The *vānaprastha* of the VasDhS is different. He combines – like the *vaikhānasa* of the GDhS – Vedic and non-Vedic elements. But the Vedic ritual element is weak: the sacrificial fire is kindled, only to be abandoned six months later.

3. *saṃnyas-*; see note 12 to chapter 2 above.

Baudhāyana Dharmasūtra (BDhS) 2.6.11.9-34 uses the designations *brahmacārin*, *gṛhastha*, *vānaprastha* and *parivrājaka*. Like the GDhS and the ĀpDhS, this portion of the BDhS accepts in the end only one *āśrama*, that of the householder (sūtra 27).

Sūtras 14-26 describe the conduct of the *vānaprastha* and *parivrājaka*. Neither of the two is credited with an interest in the true nature of the self.[4] The *vānaprastha*, now called *vaikhānasa*, is described in sūtra 15 in terms which are often identical with those of the GDhS. Here too he kindles a fire in accordance with the *Śrāmaṇaka*. The *parivrājaka*, on the other hand, keeps no fire, and no link with Vedic ritual is indicated. A
[34] further difference between the two types of ascetics, as in the GDhS, is that the *vānaprastha* does not enter the village, whereas the *parivrājaka* does, in order to beg his food.

Some passages from the MBh are of particular interest, not only because they present the two ascetic *āśrama*s as alternatives, but also because they link these two *āśrama*s to different aims. When king Pāṇḍu becomes the object of a curse as a result of which he has to abstain from sexuality, his first reaction is to decide to become a shaven ascetic (*munir muṇḍa*[*ḥ*]; MBh 1.110.7), bent on release (*mokṣam eva vyavasyāmi*; 1.110.6), equal-minded to all breathing creatures (11), begging for his food and thinking neither good nor ill of those who cause him pleasure or pain (14).[5] His two wives, however, oppose this

4. BDhS 2.6.11.26, only found here in the mss. containing Govindasvāmin's commentary, has the following enigmatic reading: *apavidhya vaidikāni karmāṇy ubhayataḥ paricchinnā madhyamaṃ padaṃ saṃśliṣyāmaha iti vadantaḥ*. BÜHLER (1882: 260) translates: "(Ascetics shall) say, 'Renouncing the works taught in the Veda, cut off from both (worlds), we attach ourselves to the central sphere (Brahman).'" It is not certain that 'the central sphere' is Brahman. GOMBRICH (1992: 173) wonders whether there is here an allusion to the Buddhists. (Added in the 2nd edition:) The analysis of this passage by TSUCHIDA (1996a) does not confirm GOMBRICH's conjecture.

5. This story of Pāṇḍu is analyzed in SHEE, 1986: 144 f.

decision, pointing out that there are other *āśrama*s, *āśrama*s which he can undertake together with his two wives, practising asceticism, and which permit him to obtain heaven (1.110.26). Pāṇḍu then decides rather to become a *vānaprastha* (34); this implies, among other things, living in the forest, surviving on fruits and roots, making offerings in the fire twice daily, matting his hair, etc., all this until his body is finished (1.110.30-35).

The plural of *āśrama* in verse 26 shows that there were at least three *āśrama*s for the author of this passage. Two of these are described: that of the shaven *muni* and that of the long-haired *vānaprastha*. Pāṇḍu has the freedom to choose between them, which shows that they are alternatives rather than successive stages. Indeed, the fact that Pāṇḍu plans to be *vānaprastha* until his body is finished confirms this.[6]

The *vānaprastha* makes offerings in the fire and betrays thus [35]
his link with the Vedic sacrificial tradition. The *muni* does nothing of the sort, and does not appear to have any link whatsoever with the Vedic fire. What is more, his aim is liberation (*mokṣa*), whereas Pāṇḍu as *vānaprastha* soon wins the road to heaven by his own power (*sārthaḥ svargasya,* 1.110.26; *svargaṃ gantuṃ parākrāntaḥ svena vīryeṇa,* 1.111.2).

The same distinction is presented in Adhyāya 9 of the Śāntiparvan (12), where Yudhiṣṭhira makes known his intention to leave the world. His first option is described in verses 4-11. It implies living in the jungle (*araṇya*), eating fruits and roots (4), pouring oblations in the fire, fasting, having matted hair (5), and satisfying ancestors and gods (10). The second option is dealt with in verses 12-29: Verse 12 begins, very appropriately, with the words *atha vā* 'alternatively'. If one follows this option one becomes a shaven ascetic (*munir muṇḍaḥ*) who lives by begging (*caran bhaikṣyam*; 12, 23) and abandons all attachments (28-29). The connection of the *parivrājaka* with liberation is also clearly

6. SHEE (1986: 166 f., esp.174) draws attention to the discussion between Yayāti and Aṣṭaka (MBh 1.86.1 – 87.3) which deals with the four *āśrama*s without introducing the idea of temporal order.

expressed in MBh 12.185.6, which speaks of the *mokṣāśrama*. The preceding discussion of the *vānaprastha* makes no mention of liberation: the *vānaprastha* can merely "conquer worlds that are hard to conquer" (12.185.2: ... *jayel lokāṃś ca durjayān*).

The story of Mudgala (MBh 3.246-247) is of particular interest, even though it does not use the terms *āśrama*, *vānaprastha* and *parivrāja(ka)*. Mudgala follows the rules of the life-style by gleaning ears of corn (*śiloñchavṛtti*) in such a manner that a place in heaven is offered to him. Considering the (few) disadvantages connected with accepting this offer, he rejects it, abandons this life-style, and turns to *dhyānayoga,* which allows him access to *nirvāṇa,* which is eternal. It is to be recalled that
[36] the *śiloñchavṛtti* characterizes certain *vānaprastha*s (such as the 'Vedic' *vānaprastha* in ĀpDhS 2.9.22.10) and ascetic householders (e.g. BDhS 3.1.7; see ch. 6 below), and that this life-style leads to heaven according to the present passage. Liberation (*nirvāṇa*) requires a different practice, which our passage refers to by the term *dhyānayoga*.

A similar contrast opposes Vyāsa, the 'author' of the MBh, to his son Śuka. Vyāsa practises asceticism for various this-worldly purposes such as, indeed, obtaining a son (MBh 12.310-311). The son has different interests: he takes no pleasure in 'the three *āśrama*s that are based on the state of the householder' and looks for liberation instead (12.311.27).[7]

To conclude one more passage from the MBh which presents the four *āśrama*s as alternatives: MBh 12.226.4-5 speaks of a Brahmin who must, after studying the Vedas, choose one of the four *āśrama*s, viz., by producing offspring and [taking] a wife, by *brahmacarya* (?), in the forest in the presence of a teacher, or by accepting the duties of a *yati*.[8]

7. Cf. SULLIVAN, 1990: 40 f.

8. MBh 12.226. 4-5:

ācāryeṇābhyanujñātaś caturṇām ekam āśramam /
ā vimokṣāc charīrasya yo 'nutiṣṭhed yathāvidhi //
prajāsargeṇa dāraiś ca brahmacaryeṇa vā punaḥ /

Mention may here be made of *Arthaśāstra* 1.3.9-12, which briefly enumerates the special duties (*svadharma*; 1.3.5) of the *gṛhastha*, *brahmacārin*, *vānaprastha* and *parivrājaka*, in this order. The order suggests already that these four *āśramas* – the term is used in 1.3.4 – are alternatives and imply no sequence. This is confirmed by the description of the duties of the *brahmacārin*; these include "residing till the end of his life with the preceptor or, in his absence, with the preceptor's son or with a fellow-*brahmacārin*" (1.3.10: *ācārye prāṇāntikī vṛttis tad-* [37]
abhāve guruputre sabrahmacāriṇi vā; tr. KANGLE, modified).[9] The duties of the *vānaprastha* include the performance of the *agnihotra*; this shows that the present account agrees by and large with the accounts of the GDhS and BDhS. And indeed, the discovery of the self does not figure in the list of duties of the *parivrājaka*.

The fifteenth chapter of the *Ahirbudhnya Saṃhitā* contains an interesting description of the four *āśramas*. This text is quite explicit about the fact that one chooses just one of the four *āśramas* after the completion of one's Vedic studies.[10] At this stage one can choose to become a *brahmacārin*, a *gṛhastha*, a *vanastha*, or a *parivrāj* (the terms *saṃnyāsa*, *saṃnyāsin*, etc. are again not used). Of particular interest is AhS 15.18, according to which only the householder keeps a Vedic fire, the other three being without.[11] AhS 15.56 specifies this for the *vanastha*: "Worshiping the fire outside or inside himself, sacrifice is his principal object."[12] The *parivrāj* has made the fires rise up (in him) (*samāropy*[*a*] ... *agnī*[*n*]; 15.62). We must conclude that

---

vane gurusakāśe vā yatidharmeṇa vā punaḥ //

9. Cf. KANGLE, 1986: III: 151.
10. AhS 15.43cd – 44ab: *vedasnāyī vratasnāyī gurave dakṣiṇāṃ dadat / prāpyānujñāṃ guror icchec caturṇām ekam āśramam /*
11. AhS 15.18: *agnimān bahumātrāvān ekaḥ kauṭumba āśramaḥ / vratādiniratāḥ śuddhās trayo 'nye 'nagnayaḥ smṛtāḥ //*
12. AhS 15.56cd: *bahir ātmani vāpy agniṃ juhvad yajñaparāyaṇaḥ.*

the institutions of *vanastha* and *parivrāj* in the AhS are already touched by the sacrificial element, as they are in most of the texts under consideration. One distinction between the *vanastha* and the *parivrāj* – the most important one, to judge by the ĀpDhS – is however preserved in the AhS: the *vanastha* occupies himself with asceticism ('the three mortifications' *trīṇi tapāṃsi*; 15.57) and reduces his activity (*vṛttisaṃkocakṛt*;
[38] 15.58), whereas the *parivrāj* searches the highest self (*anvīkṣamāṇaḥ sūkṣmaṃ ca paramātmānam ātmanā*; 15.64) and is less concerned with *tapas*.

It seems beyond doubt that the texts considered in this chapter present in their ascetic *āśrama*s a mixture of elements belonging to originally different ways of life. Most fortunately the ĀpDhS, the MŚS and some early Saṃnyāsa Upaniṣads have preserved relatively uncontaminated descriptions of those earlier ways of life which enable us to disentangle the different elements.

The confusion is not hard to explain. One important reason is that *saṃnyāsa* belongs to the end of life, and that the 'Vedic' *vānaprastha* must keep the Vedic fire, and should therefore really be married. The *āśrama*s, on the other hand, were originally alternatives, each of which could be chosen rather early in life. The two divisions would obviously not go very well together.

One would expect that the two forms of Vedic asceticism presented in our texts – that of the 'Vedic' *vānaprastha* and of the *saṃnyāsin* – would tend to transmogrify the *āśrama*s so as to become a sequence. We know that indeed all later texts do present us the *āśrama*s as a sequence of stages in the life of a high-caste Hindu. The next chapter will study how exactly this came about.

Chapter 4. The four *āśrama*s as sequence [39]

We have studied above the portion of the BDhS that deals with the *brahmacārin*, *gṛhastha*, *vānaprastha* and *parivrājaka*. The term *saṃnyāsa* is not used here, for good reasons as we have come to think. *Saṃnyāsa* is dealt with in another portion of the BDhS, kaṇḍikās 2.10.17 and 18. The beginning of this section reads:

2.10.17.1: *athātaḥ saṃnyāsavidhiṃ vyākhyāsyāmaḥ*
After this we will explain the rule of *saṃnyāsa*.

2.10.17.2: *so 'ta eva brahmacaryavān pravrajatīty ekeṣām*
According to some, he wanders forth from this very [state], practising chastity.

The *ataḥ* in these two sūtras evidently refers back to the preceding section, which deals with the householder 'desirous of offspring'. Others disagree:

2.10.17.3: *atha śālīnayāyāvarāṇām anapatyānām*
But [according to others, *saṃnyāsa*] belongs to Śālīnas and Yāyāvaras, who are childless.

2.10.17.4: *vidhuro vā prajāḥ svadharme pratiṣṭhāpya vā*
Or he is a widower; or he has established his children in their dharma.[1]

2.10.17.5: *saptatyā ūrdhvaṃ saṃnyāsam upadiśanti* [40]
They prescribe *saṃnyāsa* after [the age of] seventy.

2.10.17.6: *vānaprasthasya vā karmavirāme*
Or [*saṃnyāsa* is fit] for the *vānaprastha* when he abstains from [sacrificial] activity.

1. It is not necessary to read the gerund *pratiṣṭhāpya* with the following sentence, as does BÜHLER (1882: 273); this may be an independent gerund clause, not infrequent in late Vedic and later Sanskrit; see BRONKHORST, 1991.

These sūtras clearly look upon *saṃnyāsa* as something that takes place in old age, as indeed it should. But they also betray uncertainty about its prerequisites. 'Some' think there are no special requirements; but the general tendency expressed by these sūtras rather seems to be that a period of chastity must precede *saṃnyāsa*. Sūtra 6 mentions the *vānaprastha* in this context. This may, but does not necessarily imply that these sūtras are familiar with a system of consecutive *āśrama*s. (It is true that sūtras 15 and 16 mention the passage 'from *āśrama* to *āśrama*' (*āśramād āśramam*); but both times these terms occur in quotations, which – in the case of the composite BDhS in which "even the first two Praśnas are not quite free from interpolations" (BÜHLER, 1882: XXXV) – might conceivably be interpolations.)

Following sūtras describe how the sacred fires are deposited in the renouncer (esp. 2.10.17.21, 25; 18.8). This, of course, is essential to *saṃnyāsa*. But other sūtras emphasize the importance of the self, and its identity with Brahman (2.10.17.40; 18.9). This suggests that (Vedic) *saṃnyāsa* and the (non-Vedic) endeavour of finding the true self had become linked up.

As pointed out above, it is not certain that this portion of the BDhS knows the *āśrama*s as stages of life. Even if it doesn't, certain features of its description of *saṃnyāsa* show that it was
[41] but a small step removed from that notion.

With the *Manusmṛti* we come to a text that presents us the four *āśrama*s as four successive stages. It is also a text in which the confusion of features has become inextricable. The third *āśrama* in particular unites virtually all the features of the two Vedic and two non-Vedic forms of asceticism which we have come to distinguish.

Entering the third *āśrama*, one may take his wife with him, but this is optional (6.3); one does bring the sacred fire to the new abode (6.4) in order to perform certain specified sacrifices (6.9 f.). Forms of fasting and mortification are prescribed throughout the section concerned. All this fits in general outline what we know about the 'Vedic' *vānaprastha* of the ĀpDhS. However, Manu 6.25 then tells us that the ascetic concerned – who is supposedly still in the third *āśrama* – deposits the sacred fires in himself, and lives on without fire and without house. This rather fits the renouncer of chapter 2, above. We learn subsequently in Manu 6.29 that the ascetic occupies himself with Upaniṣadic texts for the perfection of the self (*ātmasaṃsiddhaye*); this concern with the self reminds us of the *parivrāja* of the ĀpDhS. The activity which typifies the non-Vedic *vānaprastha* of the ĀpDhS, finally, is prescribed in Manu 6.31: "Or he should set out in a north-easterly direction and walk straight forward, diligently engaged in eating nothing but water and air, until his body collapses" (tr. DONIGER and SMITH).

There can be no doubt that the *Manusmṛti* is a composite text. This does not change the fact that its section on the third *āśrama* unites features which – if our analysis is correct – belonged originally to four clearly distinct ways of life.

The fourth *āśrama* does somewhat better, but not much. It is [42]
clear that the ascetic in this *āśrama* strives to obtain liberation (*mokṣa*; 6.35f.),[2] and that the way to obtain it is knowledge of the self (6.49, 65). But he also deposits the fires in himself (6.38), and practises *tapas* (6.70, 75).

Most interestingly, even the *Manusmṛti* does not yet identify the fourth *āśrama* with *saṃnyāsa*; this has been pointed out by OLIVELLE (1981: 270 f.; 1984: 132 f.). Manu distinguishes also a so-called *vedasaṃnyāsika* (6.86),[3] who gives up ritual activity, but does not leave home: he lives peacefully under the protection of this son (*putraiśvarye sukhaṃ vaset*; 6.95). That is to say, in spite of the confusion that is already noticeable in the *Manusmṛti*, this text preserves some of the earlier distinctions.

2. Sometimes (e.g., 6.44) this ascetic is referred to as already liberated; cf. OLIVELLE, 1984: 132.

3. DONIGER and SMITH (1991: 126 n.) call this "a troubling verse" and point out that of the verses that follow it "only in 6.94-6 is such an ascetic described".

Chapter 5. Conclusions of Part I [43]

With the *Manusmṛti* we have arrived at the classical exposition of the four *āśrama*s; it is not necessary to pursue the development of this institution any further. The preceding chapters have shown that the development of the classical *āśrama* system – in as far as it concerns its two final stages – is the story of an ever increasing intermixture of elements which at one time belonged to four clearly distinguishable, and distinguished, forms of ascetic life. Two of these four show no signs of having any inherent connection with the Vedic sacrificial tradition: they are the path of mortification and the path of insight, both of which have an intimate link with the belief in rebirth as a result of one's actions. The other two forms of ascetic life preceding the classical *āśrama* system **are** connected with the Vedic sacrificial tradition, but their link to each other is less evident. There is, on the one hand, the Vedic *vānaprastha,* who lives the life of a sacrificer, but with a number of additional restrictions and mortifications. And on the other hand there is the renunciation (*saṃnyāsa*) of the aged sacrificer, who renounces everything including his sacrificial habits; only his fires he keeps, but in a different form: they are interiorized.

There is one undoubtedly Vedic feature that pervades the life of all theses different ascetics: Vedic recitation. The fact that all the texts we have considered so far are Brahmanical texts, has certainly something to do with this. But it would be a mistake to brush, on this ground, the significance of recitation aside.
Recitation had a tendency to make itself independent from its [44]
sacrificial context. This tendency shows itself, for example, in a chapter of the *Taittirīya Āraṇyaka*[1] – called *svādhyāyabrāhmaṇa*

1. Text, translation and study in MALAMOUD, 1977.

by its commentators – and in the *Jāpakopākhyāna* of the *Mahābhārata* (12.189-193).[2] Recitation – of a *saṃhitā,* as in the *Jāpakopākhyāna,* or of selected Vedic and non-Vedic mantras – made its way into the ascetic and meditative traditions of India, so much so that its original link with Vedic religion became soon obscured. The details of this development cannot here be traced.[3] But we should be aware that the mention of recitation (*svādhyāya, japa*) in a certain text does not necessarily imply that the form of asceticism with which it is connected is of Vedic origin.

2. See BEDEKAR, 1964; and PADOUX, 1987: 119.
3. BIARDEAU (1964: 106) contrasts the meanings of the term *svādhyāya* in Mīmāṃsā and Nyāya on the one hand, and in Yoga on the other.

Part II

Vedic asceticism and the sacrificial tradition

Chapter 6. Vedic asceticism [45]

We have so far limited our attention to the ascetic *āśrama*s as they are presented in the earliest texts that mention them, without asking where these forms of asceticism came from. In the case of the two forms of non-Vedic asceticism this question may be difficult to answer. We know, to be sure, that these forms of asceticism were not confined to orthodox Brahmanism; on the contrary, it is no more than reasonable to think that the forms of non-Vedic asceticism which we have discerned had a non-Vedic origin, from which both the Brahmanical texts considered above and certain non-Brahmanical movements – prominent among them the Jainas – drew their inspiration. But the absence of textual evidence does not allow us at present to say more about this.

Saṃnyāsa falls in a different category. Its link with the Vedic sacrificial tradition is sufficiently clear from the passages studied in chapter 2, above. Yet it is doubtful whether one can speak of an inherent link between *saṃnyāsa* and Vedic religion. If it is true, as seems likely, that *saṃnyāsa* evolved out of the custom to deprive the aged father of his rights, or, somewhat less harshly, out of the aged father's decision to withdraw from his possessions and prerogatives, leaving them to his sons, it would be vain to search for the aspect of Vedic religion which gave rise to this institution. This is not to say that there is no
connection at all with Vedic religion. *Saṃnyāsa* took on [46]
religious forms which sanctified the separation between the *saṃnyāsin* and human society, and added a religious dimension to this incredibly hard way of ending one's life. Yet these religious forms would have to be looked upon as more or less adventitious.

The present chapter will concentrate on the question of the relationship between the 'Vedic *vānaprastha*' and Vedic religion. SPROCKHOFF (1979: 416 f.) has drawn attention to the similarities between the Vedic *vānaprastha* of the ĀpDhS and certain kinds of householder – called Śālīnas, Yāyāvaras, and Cakracaras – described in the BDhS (3.1.1f.).[1] These householders leave their house in order to settle in a hut or cottage at the end of the village (BDhS 3.1.17). There they serve the fires and offer certain sacrifices (19). They neither teach nor sacrifice for others (21). BDhS 3.2 enumerates the various ways of subsistence out of which these householders can choose. The ninth of these (3.2.16 f.) – called *siddhecchā* (or *siddhoñchā*) – is most interesting in the present context. It is reserved for him who has become tired of the (other) modes of subsistence on account of old age or disease (*dhātukṣaya*). The person who adopts this mode of subsistence must interiorize (the fires; *ātmasamāropaṇa*) and behave like a *saṃnyāsin* (*saṃnyāsivad upa-*
[47] *cāraḥ*), except for using a strainer and wearing a reddish-brown garment. This description shows that the way of life of these householders is not preparatory to that of the *vānaprastha*, as it has been claimed.[2] On the contrary, the *siddhecchā* presents itself as the mode of subsistence for those who are old and sick,

1. SPROCKHOFF, 1984: 21 f., deals in more detail with these types of householder, and criticizes VARENNE (1960: II: 81 f.), according to whom these are not *gṛhastha*s; in support of his position SPROCKHOFF refers to SCHMIDT, 1968: 635 n. 2; BODEWITZ, 1973: 298 f.; SPROCKHOFF, 1976: 117 f., 124; KANE, *History of Dharmaśāstra* II, 1, p. 641 f. One might add that the *Padārthadharmasaṅgraha* (alias *Praśastapādabhāṣya*) refers to *householders* who, with the help of riches acquired through the life-style of Śālīna and/or Yāyāvara, perform the five *mahāyajña*s; ed. DVIVEDIN p. 273. HEESTERMAN (1982), having studied the opposition Śālīna-Yāyāvara in earlier texts, thinks that in the BDhS "the basic opposition has ... been reduced to a secondary differentiation within the common category of the householder" (p. 265).
2. SPROCKHOFF, 1979: 417; 1984: 25; SCHMIDT, 1968: 635.

and therefore likely to die *as householders*. Nor is there any indication in the text that this form of life was only, or predominantly, chosen by old men; the fact that one of the sub-choices is especially recommended for the aged suggests rather that the other alternatives were preferred by younger candidates.

The BDhS is not the only early text that prescribes ascetic practices for the householder. SPROCKHOFF (1984: 25) has rightly drawn attention to the fact that gleaning corns (*śiloñcha*) – which constitutes one of the possible ways of subsistence of the 'ascetic' householders of the BDhS – is enumerated among the proper occupations (*svakarma*) of a Brahmin in the ĀpDhS (2.5.10.4). Also the *Manusmṛti* mentions this activity as an option for the householder (Manu 4.5, 10). The best householder, moreover, makes no provisions for the morrow (*aśvastanika*; Manu 4.7-8); almost the same term is used in connection with the householder in MBh 12. 235.3, which also mentions the mode of life of the pigeons (*kāpotī vṛtti*), another form of asceticism also found in the enumeration of the BDhS.

In view of the above, we cannot but agree with MALAMOUD's (1977: 60) observation: "... le *vānaprastha* n'est qu'une variété de *gṛhastha*".[3] Of course, this conclusion applies only to [48]
the *Vedic vānaprastha*, the alternative variety of *vānaprastha*, described in the ĀpDhS, who continues (or starts) his sacrificial activity here. The non-Vedic *vānaprastha* of the ĀpDhS has obviously nothing to do with the *gṛhastha*.

It is not possible here to study the origin of asceticism within the Vedic tradition. The evidence is meagre, and we would almost inevitably be led to speculate about earlier forms of the Vedic sacrifice, which is beyond the scope of this book.[4] The later history of Vedic asceticism, on the other hand, offers fewer

3. Similarly WINTERNITZ, 1926: 220-21. Some authors see in the *vānaprastha* a compromise between the life of the householder and that of the ascetic (BIARDEAU, 1981: 38; SULLIVAN, 1990: 43), but this does no justice to his historical position.

4. See, e.g., HEESTERMAN, 1982.

difficulties. It is clear how the Vedic *vānaprastha* could come to be looked upon as constituting a separate *āśrama*. Originally his activities differed in no way from those of certain kinds of householders. The influence from non-Vedic forms of asceticism led to the assimilation of what we have called the non-Vedic *vānaprastha* on the one hand, and the more ascetically inclined householders on the other. These householders now came to be distinguished from their more worldly colleagues. However, the break between householder and *vānaprastha* was never complete; the ĀpDhS, the BDhS, the *Manusmṛti* and parts of the MBh – all of which know the four *āśrama*s, the last two even in their later, consecutive form – still preserve rules that pertain to ascetic householders.

It seems clear, then, that the *āśrama* of the Vedic *vānaprastha* is essentially a redesignation of a form of life which before that had been – and to some extent remained – an option for the Vedic householder. At best it emphasizes and enlarges
[49] certain elements which were not unknown to the observant Vedic Brahmin. The ascetic element, in particular, is not at all foreign to the Vedic sacrificial tradition. The execution of a sacrifice demands from the sacrificer (*yajamāna*) various restrictions.[5] G.U. THITE (1975: 193 f.) enumerates and illustrates, on the basis of Brāhmaṇa passages, restrictions concerning food – according to some a complete fast may be required –, sexual abstinence, limitations of speech – e.g., complete silence until sunset –, restricted movements, and various other rules. Similar restrictions are mentioned in the Śrautasūtras. The ĀpŚS

5. The consecration (*dīkṣā*) of the sacrificer has repeatedly been studied; see, e.g., LINDNER, 1878; CALAND and HENRY, 1906: 11 ff.; OLDENBERG, 1917: 397 f.; HAUER, 1922: 65 f.; KEITH, 1925: 300 f.; GONDA, 1965: 315 ff. KNIPE (1975: 124), who is aware of the ascetic element of Vedic religion, claims without justification that "a renunciant tradition ... was certainly an important dimension of brāhmaṇical orthopraxy well before the advent of the heterodox schools".

takes a rather extreme position in the following passage:[6] "When the consecrated sacrificer (*dīkṣita*) has become thin, he is pure for the sacrifice. When nothing is left in him, he is pure for the sacrifice. When his skin and bones touch each other, he is pure for the sacrifice. When the black disappears from his eyes, he is pure for the sacrifice. He begins the *dīkṣā* being fat, he sacrifices being thin."

This link with the Vedic *dīkṣā* remains visible in some of the later texts. The BDhS, for example, speaks of the *dīkṣās* of the forest dwellers.[7] Certainly not by coincidence these *dīkṣās* include the restriction of food to roots and fruit (*kandamūlaphalabhakṣa*; 3.3.3), to what comes by chance (*pravṛttāśin*; 9, [5
11), to water (*toyāhāra*; 13) and to wind (*vāyubhakṣa*; 14), restraints which we know characterize the life of the *vānaprastha* (both 'Vedic' and 'non-Vedic') in the ĀpDhS. Also the MBh (e.g., 5.118.7; 12.236.14), the *Manusmṛti* (6.29) and the *Ahirbudhnya Saṃhitā* (15.58) use the term *dīkṣā* in connection with forest-dwellers. One passage of the MBh (12.66.7) goes to the extent of calling the stage of life of the forest-dweller *dīkṣāśrama*, which confirms our impression that this way of life constitutes one permanent *dīkṣā*.[8] The observation in the MBh (12.185.1.1) that forest-dwellers pursue the Dharma of Ṛṣis is also suggestive in this connection.[9]

6. ĀpŚS 10.14.9-10: *yadā vai dīkṣitaḥ kṛśo bhavaty atha medhyo bhavati / yadāsminn antar na kiṃcana bhavaty atha medhyo bhavati / yadāsya tvacāsthi saṃdhīyate 'tha medhyo bhavati / yadāsya kṛṣṇaṃ cakṣuṣor naśyaty atha medhyo bhavati / pīvā dīkṣate / kṛśo yajate /.*
7. BDhS 3.3.15: *vaikhānasānāṃ vihitā daśa dīkṣāḥ*. The word *vaikhānasa* here is obviously a synonym of *vānaprastha* in sūtra 3.3.1.
8. Cf. MALAMOUD, 1989: 65. MALAMOUD (1976: 185) observes that the life of the *brahmacārin*, too, is one long *dīkṣā*. The extension from temporary abstinences to a permanent life of asceticism is not unknown outside India; see, e.g., W. BURKERT's (1985: 303-04) remarks on this phenomenon in Greek religion.
9. Compare this with BIARDEAU's (1976: 35) observation that many Ṛṣis that appear in the classical mythical texts – who live in the forest with

We find some evidence for Vedic asceticism in the Vedic texts themselves. Take for example RV 1.179, which contains a discussion between Agastya and his wife Lopāmudrā. THIEME (1963) has drawn attention to the fact that Agastya and Lopāmudrā live a life of celibacy, and that this was apparently not uncommon among Vedic seers 'who served truth' (*ṛtasāp*).[10]

Another example is AB 7.13 (33.1), which has a corresponding passage in ŚŚS 188-89 (15-17). We find here the following stanzas:[11]

[51]
> By means of a son have fathers always crossed over the deep darkness, since he was born as [their] self from [their] self. He is a [ship] provided with food, that carries over [to the other shore].
>
> What is the use of dirt, what of an antelope-skin? What is the use of a beard, what of asceticism? Wish for a son, O Brahmins, ...

The mention of an antelope-skin confirm that the ascetics here criticized are Vedic ascetics: also the *dīkṣita* is associated with an antelope-skin.[12]

Similar criticism is expressed in a śloka cited in the *Śatapatha Brāhmaṇa*:[13] "Durch das Wissen steigen sie dort hinauf, wo die Begierden überwunden sind. Dorthin gelangen weder Opferlöhne noch unwissende Asketen."

---

wife and children, completely absorbed in their ritual observances, their fires, their Vedic recitation – correspond rather well to the descriptions of the *vānaprastha*. An example of such a Ṛṣi is Vyāsa; see SULLIVAN, 1990: 27 ff.

10. See also O'FLAHERTY, 1973: 52 f.
11. *śaśvat putreṇa pitaro 'tyāyan bahulaṃ tamaḥ / ātmā hi jajña ātmanaḥ sa irāvaty atitāriṇī // kiṃ nu malaṃ kim ajinam kim u śmaśrūṇi kiṃ tapaḥ / putraṃ brahmāṇa icchadvaṃ ... //*
12. See, e.g., CALAND-HENRY, 1906: 21; OLDENBERG, 1917: 398 f.; FALK, 1986: 20 f.
13. ŚB 10.5.4.16: *vidyayā tad ārohanti yatra kāmāḥ parāgatāḥ / na tatra dakṣiṇā yanti nāvidvāṃsas tapasvina*[*ḥ*] //. Tr. HORSCH, 1966: 136.

The fact that the Vedic ascetics are here criticized suggests that, within the Vedic tradition itself, there existed a certain opposition between practising ascetics and those who felt that asceticism should not go too far. This impression is confirmed by numerous passages from the MBh.

Consider first the story of Jaratkāru, which the MBh presents in two versions.[14] The for us important part of the story is as follows. Jaratkāru is an ascetic who abstains from sexuality, and who therefore has no son. During his wanderings he comes across his ancestors, who find themselves in an extremely disagreeable position: they hang down in a hole, heads down, attached to a rope which a rat is about to gnaw through. The [52]
reason, it turns out, is the fact that their lineage is soon to die out, this because Jaratkāru has no son. Jaratkāru learns his lesson and begets a son in the remainder of the story, which is of no further interest for our purposes.

In both versions of the story Jaratkāru and his ancestors are Yāyāvaras,[15] i.e., one of those Vedic householders who, according to the BDhS, live ascetic lives.[16] Indeed, he is said to "observe *dīkṣā*",[17] to be a "scholar of the Vedas and their branches",[18] the "greatest of Vedic scholars".[19] The longer version makes clear that Jaratkāru is an *agnihotrin,* one who never fails to perform the *agnihotra* sacrifice.[20] Even more interesting is the self-professed aim of Jaratkāru's ascetic life-

14. MBh 1.13.9-44; and 1.41.1 – 1.44.22. See SHEE, 1986: 31-73.

15. MBh 1.13.10, 14; 1.34.12; 1.41.16. Jaratkāru is *brahmacārin* according to 1.13.19; 41.12.

16. See above.

17. *caran dīkṣām*; MBh 1.41.2.

18. *vedavedāṅgapāragaḥ*; MBh 1.41.18. The same term is used to describe his son at MBh 1.13.38. (Here and occasionally elsewhere I follow the translation by VAN BUITENEN.)

19. *mantravidāṃ śreṣṭhas*; MBh 1.43.4.

20. MBh 1.43.13-20.

style: he wishes to carry his body whole to the world hereafter.[21] SHEE (1986: 48, with note 83) draws quite rightly attention to the fact that this aim is known to accompany the Vedic sacrifice.

It is clear from this story – as it was from the AB passage discussed above, and from other MBh passages still to follow –
[53] that the ascetic life-style which evolved within the Vedic tradition was not accepted by all.[22] Or rather, it appears that the aspect of complete sexual abstinence met with opposition from the side of those who saw the possession of a son as the sole guarantee for future well-being.

This same element recurs in connection with Agastya, an ascetic about whom a variety of stories are told in the MBh.[23] His connection with Vedic ritual is more than clear. He is the son of Mitra and Varuṇa, or simply of Varuṇa.[24] He takes an active part in the struggle between gods and demons.[25] Most significantly perhaps, he is described as performing a great sacrifice, and as undertaking a *dīkṣā* of twelve years in this connection.[26] This Agastya meets his ancestors in the same disagreeable situation as had Jaratkāru, and he too decides to beget a son.[27]

The critical attitude toward asceticism, even within the Vedic tradition, manifests itself differently in the story of

21. MBh 1.42.4: ... *śariraṃ vai prāpayeyam amutra vai.* MBh 1.13.43-44 states simply that Jaratkāru went to heaven (*svarga*) with his ancestors.
22. Cp. *Śābara Bhāṣya* 1.3.4 (p. 103): *apuṃstvaṃ pracchādayantaś cāṣṭācatvāriṃśad varṣāṇi vedabrahmacaryaṃ carivantaḥ* "Some people, with a view to conceal their want of virility, remained religious students for forty-eight years" (tr. Jha, 1933: I: 95).
23. For his occurrence in the RV, see above. For the stories told about him in the MBh, see SHEE, 1986: 74-118.
24. SHEE, 1986: 74 n. 1, 2 and 3.
25. SHEE, 1986: 74 n. 10.
26. MBh 14.95.4 f. Note the mention of antelope skins (*ajina*; 3.95.10) to characterize Agastya's form of asceticism (= Vedic asceticism). This asceticism falls nonetheless under the category *gārhasthya* (3.95.1).
27. MBh 3.94.11 f.

Yavakrī/Yavakrīta.[28] Yavakrī's connection with the Vedic tradition is beyond all doubt. His father performs the *agnihotra*.[29] He himself practises asceticism in order to obtain knowledge of the [54]
Vedas.[30] The form of asceticism he practises is itself close to the Vedic sacrifice: he heats his body by placing it near a well-lit fire.[31] He even threatens to cut off his limbs one by one and sacrifice them in the fire.[32] Ritual purity is of such importance to him that his final fall will be caused by impurity.[33] For the story of Yavakrī, too, constitutes an example of misdirected asceticism.[34]

28. SHEE, 1986: 119-143.
29. MBh 3.137.17.
30. MBh 3.135.16, 19-21.
31. MBh 3.135.16-17.
32. MBh 3.135.28: *samiddhe 'gnāv upakṛtyāṅgam aṅgaṃ hoṣyāmi*
33. MBh 3.137.13-15.
34. Interestingly, another passage of the MBh (9.39.5-6; referred to in SHEE, 1986: 124 n. 36) mentions Ārṣṭiṣeṇa who *succeeds* in obtaining knowledge of the Vedas by means of *tapas*. This passage clearly represents a position more favourable to asceticism within the Vedic tradition than the preceding one.

Chapter 7. The position of the early Upaniṣads [55]

Our analysis thus far has all but ignored the early Upaniṣads. This may seem surprising, for it is precisely these old Upaniṣads that have often been considered to contain the earliest traces of the doctrine of karma and of the views and practices that came to characterize the religious current we are studying. The earliest Upaniṣads express these new ideas in a form which closely resembles the Vedic Brāhmaṇas, which has often been interpreted to support the view that they made here their first appearance.

However, the Upaniṣads themselves admit on several occasions that these new ideas are not Vedic in origin.[1] They are then put in the mouth of Kṣatriyas, often kings. This should not induce us to believe in a supposed Kṣatriya origin of these ideas. Obviously no Brahmin could accept new ideas from Śūdras or other 'low' people, only the Kṣatriyas being in positions of sufficient authority to be taken seriously. Indeed, one of the passages concerned states quite explicitly: "This knowledge has never yet come to Brahmins before you; and therefore in all the worlds has the rule belonged to the Kṣatriya only" (ChU 5.3.7; tr. HUME, 1931: 231). In a religion in which obtaining power played such a major role, only those in the possession of even more power than the Brahmins might be considered to be able to
impart new knowledge.[2] Nothing is this way said about the real [56]
origin of the new ideas.

The new knowledge normally concerns the doctrine of karma, the true nature of the self, or both. We recognize these as

1. So CHANDRA, 1971: 322 f.
2. OLIVELLE (1992: 38) suggests that "the identification of a doctrine with a king ... may have served to signal that it was a doctrine of and for the new age, an urban doctrine suitable for the new urban culture".

the central themes of the non-Vedic religious current identified in preceding chapters. The earliest Upaniṣads, not surprisingly, present these themes in a Vedic garb. Consider, for example, the teaching by the Kṣatriya Pravāhaṇa Jaibali to the Brahmin Āruṇi Gautama in ChU 5.4-10, which follows the remark quoted above. It presents first a long series of Brāhmaṇa type identifications of a variety of objects with different aspects of the sacrificial fire. The crucial part of the teaching follows in ChU 5.10. Briefly put, it states that "those who know this (i.e., the preceding identifications), and those who worship in the forest with the thought '*tapas* is faith'", will reach Brahma. Those, on the other hand, "who in the village reverence a belief in sacrifice, merit and almsgiving" will, after a complicated journey, be reborn in the womb of a Brahmin, Kṣatriya or Vaiśya if they were of pleasant conduct, and if otherwise, in the womb of a dog, swine or Caṇḍāla.

This passage merits some comments, for it highlights the position midway between two traditions of the early Upaniṣads. It clearly knows the distinction between rebirth and liberation from rebirth. Yet it does not speak of 'liberation from rebirth' but of reaching Brahma. This choice of expression, about which more will be said below, is obviously inspired by the desire to use Vedic terminology. The further statement that this is the path of the gods confirms this.

It is even more remarkable that the liberating knowledge specified in this passage is quite different from a knowledge of the self. This is very significant. The Upaniṣads represent a
[57] development of Vedic religion in which knowledge plays an increasingly important role.[3] There is no reason to think that this development owed its origin to the non-Vedic current which we

3. This aspect of the Upaniṣads is emphasized in EDGERTON, 1929; 1965: 28 f. The continuity between Brāhmaṇas and early Upaniṣads has recently again been emphasized by H.W. TULL (1989). TULL is however mistaken in thinking that this continuity proves 'the Vedic origins of karma'. See also BOYER, 1901.

have been studying. After all, its early manifestations (in the Brāhmaṇas and esp. the AV-Saṃhitā) show no link with ideas about rebirth, liberation, and the true nature of the self. Yet both this Vedic development and the non-Vedic current concerned share the conviction that certain kinds of knowledge, or insight, are quite essential for reaching their respective goals. The Upaniṣads appear to bear witness to the interaction that took place between these two originally completely distinct religious currents.[4] The passage just considered borrows the non-Vedic aim of liberation from rebirth, puts it in a Vedic garb, and offers it as reward for a typically Vedic type of knowledge.

This same passage appears further to recommend *tapas* as leading to Brahma. BAU 6.2, which contains the same story in a somewhat different form, speaks in the present context of *truth* rather than of *tapas* (6.2.15); it enumerates *tapas* among the [58]
activities that lead to rebirth in this world (6.2.16). The ambiguous position of *tapas*, which has a role to play in both traditions, Vedic and non-Vedic, accounts no doubt for its different evaluation in these two otherwise parallel texts.

In BAU 2.1 (and in slightly different form KU 4) it is king Ajātaśatru – clearly again a Kṣatriya – who instructs a Brahmin,

4. So essentially already WINTERNITZ (1908: 203): "*Mit dieser Priester-philosophie,* welche wir in den Brāhmaṇas und den zu ihnen gehörigen Āraṇyakas verfolgen können, und welche teils das Opfer, teils das von demselben unzertrennliche heilige Wort (das Brahman) zum höchsten Prinzip erhob und zum Urquell alles Seins machte, *wurde die ausserhalb der Priesterkreise entstandene und der priesterlichen Religion eigentlich zuwiederlaufende Lehre von dem inneren Selbst (dem Ātman) als dem Alleinseienden verquickt.* Das Resultat dieser unnatürlichen und gewaltsamen Verquickung sind die Upaniṣads." BROCKINGTON (1981: 78) observes: "So swift an acceptance [in Buddhism, Jainism, etc.] of the doctrine [of transmigration] probably conceals the fact that it was current in those circles from which the Buddha came before it penetrated orthodoxy. This is the more striking in that early Buddhism denied other basic tenets of the Upaniṣads ..." KARTTUNEN (1989: 154) remarks: "As far as Buddhism and the Upaniṣads represent the same trend at all, the latter are an orthodox compromise."

(Dṛpta-)Bālāki Gārgya. The teaching concerns the '*puruṣa* consisting of consciousness', identical with Brahman, and from which "all vital energies (*prāṇa*), all worlds, all gods, and all beings come forth". The knowledge here imparted concerns the true nature of the self, yet it is not presented as liberating knowledge. Contrary to ChU 5.4-10, considered above, the present passage has only borrowed, and adjusted, the liberating knowledge, but not the idea of liberation. The borrowed piece of knowledge – concerning the true nature of the self – has, to be sure, been adjusted to its new surroundings. The self is equated with the Brahmanical concept of Brahman, the source of all there is. In a way this identification is a continuation, even the culmination, of the identifications which characterize the Brāhmaṇas and other Vedic texts. At the same time this supreme identification Brahman = self constituted an almost natural inlet for the non-Vedic ideas into orthodox Vedism. The fact that, here too, the teaching is put in the mouth of a Kṣatriya, indicates that we are not alone in thinking that in this passage non-Vedic ideas are being introduced.

In ChU 5.11-18, once again, a group of learned Brahmins have to ask a Kṣatriya – king Aśvapati Kaikeya – to instruct them on the true nature of our *ātman* and of Brahman. Interestingly, here too no mention is made of liberation from rebirths. Note further that the king is not presented as a revolutionary: the
[59] Brahmins have to wait, upon their arrival, for the king is about to perform a sacrifice! The idea of a Kṣatriya 'revolt' against the Brahmins is therefore in patent opposition to this passage.

BAU 3.2.13 is another example of a passage which introduces only the new doctrine of karma, without speaking about knowledge of the real nature of the self, nor indeed of liberation.[5] This time the new teaching is put in the mouth of the ancient sage Yājñavalkya, who refuses, to be sure, to speak of it

5. It is not clear either whether the passage speaks of rebirth in the ordinary sense of the term; this was pointed out by SCHRADER (1910).

in public. It seems clear that we face here another way used to convince the Brahmins of the respectability, and this time also of the Brahmin origin, of the new ideas: they are not here attributed to Kṣatriyas, but to an ancient and respected sage.[6]

Interestingly, this same Yājñavalkya finds himself a little later (BAU 3.5) involved in a discussion regarding the true nature of the self, which is Brahman. The result of knowing the *ātman* is described as follows:[7] "It is this *ātman,* I say, which when they know, Brahmins abjure the desire for sons, the desire for possessions, the desire for [heavenly] worlds, and take up the begging ascetic's life". We recognize in the begging ascetic who knows the self, or strives to obtain knowledge of the self, the non-Vedic wandering ascetic of the ĀpDhS and elsewhere. Clearly this form of asceticism was known to the author of this portion of the BAU. This passage further bears witness to the fact that non-Vedic asceticism was already practised by [60]
Brahmins. There is every reason to think that these Brahmins lived this kind of life in order to attain liberation, even though the present passage of the BAU says nothing to that effect.

There is no need to discuss in detail all the Upaniṣadic passages that introduce the new ideas. One more passage (BAU 4.4.22) will here be cited which expresses explicitly the crucial doctrine that the real self does not take part in any action:[8] "Verily, he is the great, unborn Soul, who is this [person] consisting of

6. It is impossible to believe, with BASHAM, 1989: 43 f., that this passage shows that Yājñavalkya invented the doctrine of karman, which he here still held secret but subsequently discussed in public. Yājñavalkya, be it noted, is already an old man in ŚB 3.8.2.25.
7. BAU 3.5.1: *etaṃ vai tam ātmānaṃ viditvā brāhmaṇāḥ putraiṣaṇāyāś ca vittaiṣaṇāyāś ca lokaiṣaṇāyāś ca vyutthāyātha bhikṣācaryaṃ caranti;* tr. EDGERTON, 1965: 141.
8. BAU 4.4.22: *sa vā eṣa mahān aja ātmā yo 'yaṃ vijñānamayaḥ prāṇeṣu / ... / sa na sādhunā karmaṇā bhūyān no evāsādhunā kanīyān /*. Tr. HUME, 1931: 143, modified.

knowledge among the senses. ... He does not become greater by good action nor inferior by bad action."

The non-Vedic ideas do not only make their appearance in the Upaniṣads. As an example we consider *Jaiminīya Brāhmaṇa* 1.17-18,[9] which has its own way of integrating the new ideas. This passage mentions, and accepts, both rebirth and the continuation of life in one's son. In order to make this possible the existence of two selves is propounded. The self of the human world is reborn in the womb of the wife, whereas the self of the divine world is carried towards the sun by the sacrificial and funerary fire. There this second self must answer the question 'who are you?' If he merely mentions his name and the name of his family, he is sent back. (The text is not completely clear, but the expression "Night and day overtake his world" (*tasya hāhorātre lokam āpnutaḥ*) suggests that this self returns to the world of days and nights, i.e., to the world of mortals.) If, on the other hand, he proclaims his identity with the God Prajāpati, he
[61] "approaches the essence of good deeds" (*sa etam eva sukṛtarasam apyeti*).

The essential elements of the new doctrine are present: One will be reborn in this world, unless one knows the true nature of one's self. These elements are, here again, put in a Vedic garb which, this time, allows also for the Vedic belief in continued life in one's son.

The concern with the true nature of the self that we find so often in these and other passages leaves no doubt that their authors must have felt akin to the life-style of the *parivrāja* of the ĀpDhS. And indeed, a number of Upaniṣadic passages confirm this. BAU 4.4.22, for example, states in connection with the *ātman*:[10] "Such a one the Brahmins desire to know by

9. Translated in BODEWITZ, 1973: 52 f.

10. BAU 4.4.22: *tam etaṃ vedānuvacanena brāhmaṇā vividiṣanti yajñena dānena tapasā 'nāśakena / etam eva viditvā munir bhavati / etam eva pravrājino lokam icchantaḥ pravrajanti / ... te ha sma ... bhikṣācaryaṃ caranti* /. Tr. HUME, 1931: 143, modified.

repetition of the Vedas, by sacrifices, by offerings, by penance, by fasting. On knowing him, in truth, one becomes a *muni*. Desiring him only as their home, wandering ascetics (*pravrājin*) wander forth. ... They live the life of a mendicant." The *pravrājin* of this passage and the *parivrāja* of the ĀpDhS have in common their wandering life-style, their habit to beg for food, their concern with the true nature of the self. BAU 3.5, too, explains that Brahmins who know the Self live the life of mendicants (*bhikṣācaryaṃ caranti*).

The new doctrines that make their appearance in the early Upaniṣads – and which, I propose, were borrowed from non-Vedic currents – did not radically change the Vedic tradition. The Upaniṣads remained, quite on the contrary, marginal. They continued a tradition of their own which, as time went by, became ever more outspoken in its criticism of the Vedic sacri- [62]
ficial tradition. The *Muṇḍaka Upaniṣad* (1.2.7 f.), to cite but one example, states that only fools consider the Vedic sacrifices the best means; they will obtain old age and death all over again.[11] The orthodox – and orthoprax – Vedic tradition simply ignored its Upaniṣads, including the oldest ones. The link of the later Upaniṣads with the rest of Vedic literature became, not surprisingly, ever more tenuous. Indeed, most of them came to be assigned to the *Atharvaveda*, which shows that their Vedic nature (*śruti*) was not taken very seriously. The controversy in the commentaries on the Brahmasūtras whether *saṃnyāsa* is or is not a *śrauta āśrama*, moreover, could not have arisen if any of the Saṃnyāsa Upaniṣads had been really considered Vedic.[12] The oldest texts on Dharma rarely refer to the Upaniṣads.[13] Very

11. DESHPANDE (1990: 26) observes that the "markedly anti-ritual tendencies and a decisive preference for the ascetic and meditative way of life [in the *Muṇḍaka Upaniṣad*] may perhaps show a certain influx of non-Vedic traditions."

12. See SPROCKHOFF, 1976: 8, 22; DEUSSEN, 1887: 648 f.; THIBAUT, 1904: III: 693 f.

13. BDhS 2.10.18.15 speaks of teachers who explain the Upaniṣad

significantly, the ĀpDhS, which has a great deal to say about the different forms of asceticism, does not refer to the Upaniṣads in this context. It is true that it mentions the Upaniṣads in a different context (2.2.5.1) and cites in 1.8.22-23 lines which show some similarity with the *Kāṭhaka Upaniṣad,*[14] but this merely accentuates the fact that, in the opinion of the author of the ĀpDhS, the Upaniṣadic tradition has no direct link with any of the three forms of asceticism he describes. Later texts on Dharma mention the Upaniṣads in the context of the ascetic
[63] *āśramas*;[15] one gains the impression that their mention is meant to lend an air of orthodoxy to the ascetic practices which had originally nothing to do with Vedism.

This marginal position of the Upaniṣads does not come to an end until, many centuries later, the Vedānta system of philosophy gains enormously in popularity and manages to present the Upaniṣads as **the** expression of orthodox Vedism.[16] This development cannot be separated from the intrusion of non-Vedic asceticism into the Vedic world view, even though an enormous time gap separates the two.

To conclude this chapter, let us consider which of the ascetic life-styles studied in the earlier chapters of this book were known to the authors of the early Upaniṣads. It seems more than likely that the two forms of Vedic asceticism which we have come to discern were known to them, even if the terms *saṃnyāsa* and *vānaprastha* were not necessarily used. *Saṃnyāsa*, as we have seen, concerned the fate of the aged, and indeed, Yājñavalkya's departure (BAU 2.4; 4.5; SPROCKHOFF, 1976: 291; 1979: 396 f.; 1981: 68 f.) falls within this category. And if we

---

(*upaniṣadam ācāryā bruvate*) in the context of its description of the life of the *saṃnyāsin*.

14. NAKAMURA, 1983: 308 f.
15. So Manu 6.29, 83, 94.
16. The earliest evidence for a Vedāntic system of philosophy as an independent school appears to date from the sixth century C.E. See MESQUITA, 1991: 214-15.

are correct in thinking that the Vedic *vānaprastha* was really a householder who imposed upon himself extra restrictions, this form of life, too, may have been known to those Upaniṣads. We must however be aware that this form of life was not of much interest to the oldest Upaniṣads, for their object of real interest is the non-Vedic search for the true nature of the self. The ideal of the non-Vedic ascetic who, through cessation of activity, aspired to become freed from the effects of activity, did not find much resonance in these Upaniṣads either, and is not obviously present in them.

Chapter 8. Conclusions of Part II [64]

There is no reason to doubt that Vedic asceticism developed largely or wholly independently out of certain aspects of the Vedic sacrifice. It is certainly not impossible that this development was aided by the simultaneous existence of non-Vedic forms of asceticism, but this seems at present beyond proof. The available evidence suggests that the appearance of forms of asceticism within Vedic religion came about largely independently of anything that took place outside it.

Similar claims have been made about the ideas of rebirth and karman.[1] Here, however, the available evidence leaves ample scope for doubt. We have seen that many of the earliest passages that introduce these ideas contain themselves indications that they had a non-Brahmaṇic origin. What is more, there are numerous passages in early Indian literature – a number of them presented in different chapters of this book – which show that the ideas of rebirth and karman were associated in the Indian mind with non-Vedic currents of religion and asceticism. Most of the early Vedic passages which supposedly show the Vedic origins of these ideas concern, as HORSCH (1971: 156) correctly observed, "Universalvorstellungen, die bei den verschiedensten Völkern der Erde auftreten, ohne dort zur Seelenwanderungslehre geführt zu haben." In other words, they prove nothing. [65]

Nor does the continuity of style and content which exists between the early Upaniṣads and the earlier Brāhmaṇas prove anything about the origin of the new ideas. It merely proves that

1. See, e.g., HORSCH, 1971; WITZEL, 1984; TULL, 1989. Note on the other hand BIARDEAU's (1964: 90 n. 1) remark: "On peut donc penser que la doctrine des rites est reprise par les tenants du karman et de la délivrance qui, ce faisant, l'intègrent à leur perspective."

these ideas could only be accepted by the Brahmins in a Brahmanic garb, fully integrated into their new surroundings.[2]

2. The doctrine of karman kept having to compete with other causalities; see HALBFASS' (1991a: 291 f.) chapter "Competing causalities: karma, Vedic rituals, and the natural world".

Part III

The two traditions

Chapter 9. Kapila and the Vedic tradition [66]

In order to study the opposition that was felt in the early texts between Vedic and non-Vedic asceticism, it will be interesting first to study the figure of Kapila. Kapila is often presented as a representative of non-Vedic asceticism. Toward the end of the chapter we will study a passage in which his type of asceticism is explicitly contrasted with another type of asceticism, viz., that of Vedic ascetics.

Kapila is mentioned in an intriguing passage of the BDhS immediately after its rejection of the four *āśrama*s. Sūtra 2.6.11.28 states, in BÜHLER's translation: "With reference to this matter they quote also (the following passage): 'There was, forsooth, an Asura, Kapila by name, the son of Prahlāda. Striving with the gods, he made these divisions. A wise man should not take heed of them.'"[1] Two features of this passage call for closer attention: (i) the demoniacal nature of the sage Kapila; and (ii) the opposition here expressed between the Vedic tradition and that associated with Kapila.

(i) Kapila is, of course, primarily known as the sage who reputedly created the Sāṃkhya system of philosophy. In the classical Sāṃkhya texts he is more than just a sage; he is an [67]
incarnation of God (*īśvara*). The *Yuktidīpikā* describes him as *īśvaramaharṣi* 'great seer who is [an incorporation of] God' (BRONKHORST, 1983: 153). The *Māṭharavṛtti* speaks of "the great seer called Kapila, an incarnation of the exalted old Self, the son of Prajāpati Kardama" (id. p. 156). God is also "the light

1. BDhS 2.6.11.28: *tatrodāharanti / prāhlādir ha vai kapilo nāmāsura āsa sa etān bhedāṃś cakāra devaiḥ spardhamānas tān manīṣī nādriyeta //*. The translation deviates from BÜHLER's in substituting Asura for Āsura. See WINTERNITZ, 1926: 225; LINGAT, 1967: 66.

of Kapila" (id. p. 157). Yoga sūtras 1.24-25, moreover, describe God, who is a special kind of self, as possessing the germ of Kapila, here referred to as 'the omniscient one'; in other words, God is the self of Kapila, and Kapila an incarnation of God. This interpretation is supported by the *Yoga Bhāṣya* (BRONKHORST, 1985: 194 f.). The commentary on the *Sāṃkhyakārikā* which only survived in Paramārtha's Chinese translation tells us, under kārikā 1, that Kapila was 'born from heaven' and 'endowed with self-existence'.[2] According to the *Yuktidīpikā*, again, he – i.e., the *paramarṣi* – who gave names to things (p. 5 l. 9-10), is the first-born (*viśvāgraja*; p. 6 l. 1). Vācaspati Miśra's *Tattvavaiśāradī* on Yoga sūtra 1.25, finally, calls Kapila an *avatāra* of Viṣṇu, and adds that Kapila is identical with the self-existent Hiraṇyagarbha, and with God *(īśvara)*. Kapila's divine nature may therefore be taken as established for classical Sāṃkhya.

An inspection of the earlier texts shows that Kapila was already divine in the pre-classical period. Consider, to begin with, Aśvaghoṣa's Buddhacarita XII.20-21. Verse 20 introduces the 'field-knower' (*kṣetrajña*) and states (20cd): "Those who think about the self call the self *kṣetrajña*" (*kṣetrajña iti cātmānaṃ kathayanty ātmacintakāḥ*). Verse 21 then continues:

[68] *saśiṣyaḥ kapilaś ceha pratibuddha*[3] *iti smṛtiḥ /*
saputro 'pratibuddhas tu prajāpatir ihocyate //

This must mean:

> [This *kṣetrajña*] when having students and being Kapila is remembered in this world as the enlightened one. But when having sons and not being enlightened it is here called Prajāpati.

2. T. 2137, vol. 54, p. 1245a l. 5-6; TAKAKUSU 1904: 979.
3. JOHNSTON's most important ms. has *-buddhi,* which has been changed into *-buddhir* in the edition. This reading does not however seem to make much sense. Kapila is described as *buddha* MBh 12.290.3.

Clearly Kapila is, if anything, more elevated than Prajāpati.[4]

The *Mahābhārata* contains numerous references to Kapila, the supreme seer (*paramarṣi*). He is identified with Prajāpati (12.211.9) and with Vāsudeva (3.106.2); he is one of the mind-born sons of Brahman (12.327.64); or he is called *deva* 'god', identical with Śakradhanu, son of the sun (5.107.17). Both Nārāyaṇa and Kṛṣṇa say of themselves that the Sāṃkhya masters call them "Kapila, possessor of wisdom, residing in the sun, eternal" (12.326.64; 330.30; see also 12.43.12). Śiva is Sanat-kumāra for the Yogins, Kapila for the Sāṅkhyas (13.14.159). As propounder of Sāṃkhya, Kapila is mentioned beside Hiraṇya-garbha, who propounded Yoga (MBh 12.337.60; 326.64.65; 330.30-31).

Perhaps the earliest reference to 'the seer Kapila' occurs in *Śvetāśvatara Upaniṣad* 5.2. Modern interpreters have not infrequently preferred the translation 'tawny, red' to 'Kapila', because comparison with other verses of the ŚvetUp (3.4; 4.11-
12) shows that this seer Kapila must be identical with Hiraṇya- [69]
garbha and linked to Rudra.[5] This identity poses no problem the moment we abandon the idea that Kapila ever was an ordinary human being.

The present passage of the BDhS calls Kapila an Asura, i.e., a demon. It is to be noted that Asuras are not in principle subordinated to the gods; they are, on the contrary, often engaged in battles with the gods, battles which, it is true, the gods normally win. The fact that Kapila appears here as an Asura, is revealing. It suggests that the author of our passage of the BDhS knew Kapila as a divine being, but one who was not, in his opinion, connected with orthodox Vedism.[6]

4. It is doubtful whether Kapila Gautama, the founder of Kapilavastu according to Aśvaghoṣa's *Saundarananda* canto I, is to be identified with this Kapila.
5. See, e.g., HUME, 1931: 406 with n. 2.
6. Another instance where the term Asura appears to relate to non-Vedic Indians is discussed in Staal, 1983: I: 136 f. A similar situation may

Kapila's characterization as 'son of Prahlāda' (*prāhlādi*) is not without interest either. Prahlāda is, in the earliest texts (*Taittirīya Brāhmaṇa*, Purāṇapañcalakṣaṇa, *Mahābhārata*) the king of the Asuras (Hacker, 1959: 14 f.). This characterization, though unknown elsewhere in connection with Kapila, confirms that the latter is here indeed looked upon as an Asura. But Prahlāda is also, in a number of passages of the MBh, a teacher of wisdom, who possesses omniscience (HACKER, p. 18 f.). This suggests that his link with Kapila may have more than superficial significance. For Kapila, too, is described as possessor of wisdom, of omniscience, as we have seen.

Kapila is nowhere else, to my knowledge, explicitly de-
[70] scribed as a demon. Yet some features of early literature are suggestive in this connection. Consider first the role of Kapila in the story of Sagara and his sons (MBh 3.104-106),[7] as retold by Wendy DONIGER O'Flaherty (1980: 220 f.):

> King Sagara had two wives. In order to obtain sons, he performed asceticism ...; then, by the favor of Śiva he obtained sixty thousand sons from one wife and one son ... from the other. After some time, the king performed a horse sacrifice; as the horse wandered over the earth, protected by the king's sons, it reached the ocean, and there it disappeared. The king sent his sixty thousand sons to search for the horse; they dug with spades in the earth, destroying many living creatures, digging out the ocean that is the abode of sea demons. They reached down into Hell, and there they saw the horse wandering about, and they saw the sage Kapila haloed in flames, blazing with ascetic power. The sons were angry and behaved disrespectfully to

---

prevail in the case of the Rākṣasa Rāvaṇa, "who is elsewhere known as a prince of demons but who in this milieu (i.e., of the *Kumāratantra*) occupies the position of a tutelary deity of exorcism" (GOUDRIAAN, 1981: 128); see also GOUDRIAAN, 1977: 165 f.; J. FILLIOZAT, 1937: 159 ff. Examples of the transformation in traditional narratives of 'enemy' into 'hero' are known from elsewhere, too; see FORSYTH, 1987: 36. (Added in the 2nd edition:) Hayagrīva is an Indian example of a demonic figure who becomes divine, even an avatāra of Viṣṇu; cp. STUTLEY, 1986: 111.

7. For a study of this myth in epic-purāṇic literature, see BOCK, 1984.

> Kapila; infuriated, he released a flame from his eye and burnt all the sons to ashes. Then [Sagara's grandson] Aṃśuman came and propitiated Kapila ...

One might wonder why Kapila practises his asceticism in Hell of all places. Even more telling may be that many elements of the above myth, as O'FLAHERTY points out, recur in the story of Dhundhu (MBh 3.193-195) who, though playing a role similar to that of Kapila, is an Asura. I quote again from O'FLAHERTY (1980: 222; with modifications):

> King Bṛhadaśva had a son called Kuvalāśva, who in his turn had
> 21,000 sons. When the old king handed over his throne to Kuvalāśva [71]
> and entered the forest, he met the sage Uttaṅka, who told him that a demon named Dhundhu was performing asceticism there by his hermitage, in the sands of the ocean, burning like the doomsday fire, with flames issuing from his mouth, causing the waters to flow about him in a whirlpool. Bṛhadaśva asked Kuvalāśva to subdue the demon; his sons dug down into the sand, but Dhundhu appeared from the ocean, breathing fire, and he burnt them all with his power of asceticism. Then Kuvalāśva drank up the watery flood, quenched the fire with water, and killed the demon Dhundhu, burning him up.

The parallelism between Dhundhu and Kapila is emphasized by the MBh itself: "Dhundhu burnt the sons of Bṛhadaśva with the fire from his mouth, just as Kapila had burnt the sons of Sagara."[8]

In conclusion it may be observed that Kapila's frequent association with Āsuri might be significant: Āsuri means 'son of an Asura'.

(ii) The opposition between Kapila and the Vedic tradition finds expression in an interesting passage of the *Mahābhārata* (12.260-262) which records a discussion between Kapila and the

8. MBh 3.195.25:
mukhajenāgninā kruddho lokān udvartayann iva /
kṣaṇena rājaśārdūla pureva kapilaḥ prabhuḥ /
sagarasyātmajān kruddhas tad adbhutam ivābhavat //
tr. O'FLAHERTY.

seer (*ṛṣi*) Syūmaraśmi, in order to show that both the life of a householder and that of the renouncer (*tyāga*) result in great fruit and are both authoritative (260.2-4).[9] Syūmaraśmi sings here the glory of the Vedic way of life, with heavy emphasis on the sacrifice. He criticizes the "cessation of effort called
[72] *pravrajyā*" of the lazy (*alasa*) sages who are without faith and wisdom, devoid of subtle vision (261.10). He rejects the possibility of liberation (*mokṣa*), pointing out that mortal beings rather have to pay off their debts towards the manes, the gods, and the twice-born (261.15). And he reminds Kapila of the central position of the Brahmin; the Brahmin is the cause of the three worlds, their eternal and stable boundary (12.261.11).

Kapila, in his turn, stresses his respect for the Vedas (12.260.12: *nāhaṃ vedān vinindāmi*; 262.1: *na vedāḥ pṛṣṭhataḥ-kṛtāḥ*), but points out that the Vedas contain the two contradictory messages that one must act and that one must abstain from action (260.15). A little later he pronounces several verses which tell us what a true Brahmin is like: he guards the gates of his body – i.e., his sexual organ, stomach, arms and speech –, without which there is no use of *tapas*, sacrificing and knowing the self; the true Brahmin's requirements are very limited, he likes to be alone where all others like to live in couples, he knows the original form (*prakṛti*) and the modified forms (*vikṛti*) of all this, he knows and inspires no fear, and is the soul of all living beings.[10] Kapila then gives a description of the people of yore, who had direct knowledge of Dharma (*pratyakṣadharma*; 12.262.8) and led in general exemplary lives. They all followed one Dharma which, however, has four legs: "Those virtuous bull-like men had recourse to the four-legged Dharma; having reached it in accordance with the law, they [all] obtain the highest destiny, leaving the house, others by resorting to the forest, by becoming householders, others again as *brahma-*

9. Cf. WINTERNITZ, 1926: 225.
10. MBh 12.261.27-32.

cārins."[11] Kapila also mentions the 'fourth Upaniṣadic Dharma' [73]
(*caturtha aupaniṣado dharmaḥ*; 12.262.27) to be attained by accomplished, self-restrained Brahmins (28). We learn from ChU 2.23.1 – cited above, ch. 1 – that this fourth Dharma belongs to the man 'who resides in Brahman' (*brahmasaṃstha*), and the following verses of MBh 12.262 confirm this. The fourth Upaniṣadic Dharma is rooted in contentment, consists in renunciation, and in the search of knowledge.[12] The two following verses then speak of liberation (*apavarga*) as the eternal duty of the ascetic (*yatidharma*), and of the desire for Brahman's abode, as a result of which one is freed from the cycle of rebirths (30cd: *brahmaṇaḥ padam anvicchan saṃsārān mucyate śuciḥ*). In conclusion Kapila points out that (sacrificial) acts are a purification of the body (*śarīrapakti*; 36), whereas knowledge is the highest path. But this does not prevent him from saying (v. 41): "Those who know the Veda know all; all is rooted in the Veda, for in the Veda is the foundation of all that exists and does not exist."

Kapila, according to MBh 12.327.64-66, represents – along with certain other sages – *the nivṛtta dharma*, he is a knower of Yoga (*yogavid*) and master in the science of liberation (*mokṣaśāstre ācārya*). The group of sages to which Kapila belongs is contrasted with another group, consisting of knowers of the Veda (*vedavid*), whose *dharma* is *pravṛtti* (12.327.61-63). In MBh 12.312.4 the science of Yoga (*yogaśāstra*) which leads to liberation (3, 6, etc.) is called *kāpila* 'belonging to Kapila'.

11. MBh 12.262.19-20:
    dharmam ekaṃ catuṣpādam āśritās te nararṣabhāḥ /
    taṃ santo vidhivat prāpya gacchanti paramāṃ gatim //
    gṛhebhya eva niṣkramya vanam anye samāśritāḥ /
    gṛham evābhisaṃśritya tato 'nye brahmacāriṇaḥ //

12. MBh 12.262.28 cd: *(sa) saṃtoṣamūlas tyāgātmā jñānādhiṣṭhānam ucyate.* (Added in the 2nd edition:) For a detailed discussion of the 'fourth Upaniṣadic Dharma' in connection with ChU 2.23, see TSUCHIDA, 1996.

We now turn again to Aśvaghoṣa's Buddhacarita. This text describes, among other things, how the future Buddha acquainted himself with various forms of religious life, before
[74] he found his own way to *nirvāṇa*. Most noteworthy are his visit to the penance grove described in Sarga 7, and the instruction he receives from Arāḍa Kālāma in Sarga 12.

Arāḍa Kālāma teaches a form of Sāṃkhya and mentions in this context Kapila (see above). His aim is to reach liberation from *saṃsāra* (*yathā ... saṃsāro ... nivartate*; 12.16) through knowledge of the self.[13] We recognize this as one of the non-Vedic ways leading to final liberation.

At least as interesting are the Bodhisattva's experiences in the penance grove (*tapovana*, *āśrama*). Its inhabitants divide their time, as appears from the description, between a variety of ascetic practices and Vedic sacrifices. Very important in the present context are the reasons for which these practices are undertaken: most prominently mentioned is the obtainment of heaven (7.10, 18, 20, 21, 24, 48). Indeed, the main reason given by the Bodhisattva for leaving the *āśrama* is that he does not want heaven, but the end of rebirth. It is in this context (7.48) that he remarks that the *nivṛttidharma* is different from *pravṛtti*. *Pravṛtti* here designates the asceticism practised in the *āśrama*. The teaching of Arāḍa, on the other hand, aims at final liberation (7.52-54) and belongs to the category *nivṛttidharma*.

Here, then, Kapila's way is explicitly contrasted with the ascetic practices of the Vedic penance grove. The former is *nivṛtti*, the latter is *pravṛtti*; the former leads to liberation, the latter to heaven.

To conclude this chapter, let us note that Kapila's link with renunciation is evident also from Baudhāyana Gṛhyaśeṣasūtra 4.16, which terms the rules of becoming a *saṃnyāsin* '*Kapila-*

13. The meditative practices taught by Arāḍa (12.46 f.) are of Buddhist origin.

saṃnyāsavidhi'.[14] P.V. KANE (*History of Dharmaśāstra* II [75]
p. 953) draws attention to a line of royal kings called *nṛpati-parivrājaka* 'kingly ascetics', attested in Gupta inscriptions, whose founder is said to have been (an incarnation of) Kapila.[15] The Jaina text *Uttarādhyayana* chapter 8, which describes the virtues of asceticism, is also ascribed to Kapila. The commentary on the *Paṇṇavaṇā* describes the wandering beggars called Carakas as descendants of Kapila.[16]

Recall in this context once again that Kapila in the BDhS is the son of Prahlāda. Prahlāda, king of the Asuras, is frequently engaged in battles with Indra, king of the gods (HACKER, 1959: 16-17). But Indra is also antagonistic to the practice of asceticism, with which he interferes in various ways; Minoru HARA (1975) enumerates dissuasion, seduction by celestial nymphs, and straightforward violence, and illustrates these with passages from the MBh and from the Pāli Jātakas. Again one is tempted to interpret these stories as giving expression to an opposition which was felt to exist between orthodox Vedic religion and the tradition of wisdom and asceticism linked to the names of Prahlāda and, more in particular, Kapila.

This tradition of wisdom and asceticism is, of course, the one which we have come to distinguish from the Vedic tradition. Kapila belongs most often to that manifestation of the non-Vedic tradition which looks for liberation from the cycle of rebirths through insight into the true nature of the self. It is not necessary to recall that the Sāṃkhya philosophy, in its various forms, is precisely the school of thought that stresses the fundamentally non-active nature of the soul, which is profoundly different from the material and mental world.

14. GONDA, 1977: 589.

15. FLEET, 1970: 114-115. (Added in the 2nd edition:) SCHARFE (1987: 308) proposes a different interpretation for the term *nṛpati-parivrājaka*.

16. JAIN, 1984: 304.

Chapter 10. Śramaṇas and Brahmins [76]

We have seen in chapter 1 that Megasthenes used the terms Śramaṇa and Brahmin to refer to the two types of ascetics that we have come to distinguish. The opposition that existed between these two groups is confirmed by a passage of the second century B.C.E. in Patañjali's Mahābhāṣya (ed. Kielhorn I p. 476 l. 9; on P. 2.4.12 vt. 2), which mentions the compound *śramaṇabrāhmaṇam* to illustrate the sense *yeṣāṃ ca virodhaḥ śāśvatikaḥ* "opposition between whom is eternal".

The term Śramaṇa is little used in the Veda and in the epics.* It is, on the other hand, frequently found in the old Buddhist and Jaina canons. Indeed, the founders of these two religions are themselves referred to as Śramaṇas (*samaṇa* in Pāli and Ardhamāgadhī), as are their followers. The question to be addressed is: do these texts preserve any trace of the distinction that existed between Śramaṇas and Brahmin ascetics?

Consider first the *Aggañña Sutta* of the *Dīgha Nikāya*. While describing the history of the world, which is a history of ever increasing decline, this text relates (DN III p. 93 f.) how some beings decide to get rid (*bāhenti*) of evil. This fact is presented as an etymological explanation of the name Brahmin, which these beings obtain.[1] These Brahmins build leaf huts in [77]

* For a recent discussion, see OLIVELLE, 1993: 11 f. OLIVELLE concludes from the use of the term in some Vedic passages (essentially one: *Taittirīya Āraṇyaka* 2.7) that here the Śramaṇa is right at the centre of the Vedic tradition. However, he rightly points out that "[t]he meaning of this term ... should not be simply assumed to be the same as in ... later (and we may add: different, JB) ascetical contexts". Indeed, the preponderant use elsewhere (e.g., by Megasthenes and Patañjali) allows us to speak of a (non-Vedic) Śramaṇa movement without much risk of confusion.

1. For a comparison with the Chinese parallels, see MEISIG, 1988: 146 f.

the jungle and meditate there. They are therefore called *jhāyaka* 'meditator'. This designation distinguishes them from 'certain among them' who, incapable of meditating, become *ajjhāyaka* 'non-meditator', but also 'reciter [of the Veda]'.[2] The real Brahmins, i.e. those who meditate, are further described as follows:[3] "Extinct for them the burning coal, vanished the smoke, fallen lies pestle and mortar; gathering of an evening for the evening meal, of a morning for the morning meal, they go down into village and town and royal city, seeking food. When they have gotten food, back again in their leafhuts they meditate."

It is remarkable, and somewhat puzzling, that the Brahmin meditators are here described as without fire. Perhaps GOMBRICH (1992: 174) is right in assuming that the vital terms *vītaṅgāra*, *vītadhūma*, and *paṇṇa-* (or *sanna-*?) *musala* were borrowed from Brahmanical phraseology,[4] but twisted to suit a different purpose. We may then also have to agree that this passage was not intended to describe a single historical phenomenon. It is however clear that the present passage does not claim that Brahmin meditators, who live in leaf huts in the jungle, are a thing of the past. It is true that 'certain among

---

One of these parallels, the isolated text T. 10 (vol. 1) p. 221a esp. l. 12-13, reserves the name Brahmin for those who desist from meditating. This etymology, incidentally, indicates that some such form as *baṃhaṇa* or *bāhaṇa*, instead of *brāhmaṇa*, was in use at the time; HINÜBER, 1991: 186.

2. Richard GOMBRICH (1992, esp. p. 163) draws attention to the humoristic aspect of the 'etymology' of *ajjhāyaka*.

3. DN III p. 94: *vītaṅgārā vītadhūmā paṇṇamusalā sāyaṃ sāyamāsāya pāto pātarāsāya gāmanigamarājadhāniyo osaranti ghāsam esanā / te ghāsaṃ paṭilabhitvā punad eva araññāyatane paṇṇakuṭīsu jhāyanti /*. Tr. RHYS DAVIDS, 1921: 89.

4. BDhS 2.6.11.22 has *sannamusala* and *vyaṅgāra*, Manu 6.56 *vidhūma*, *sannamusala* and *vyaṅgāra*; here these expressions refer, not to the situation of the ascetic described, but to that of the village in which he is going to beg.

them' have abandoned this way of life, but at least some have stuck to it. This is interesting, for the next page describes the origin of the Śramaṇas:[5] "Now there came a time, Vāseṭṭha, [78]
when some Khattiya, misprizing his own norm, went forth from home into the homeless life, saying: I will become a Śramaṇa. Some Brahmin too did the same, likewise some Vessa and some Sudda, each finding some fault in his particular norm. Out of these four groups, Vāseṭṭha, the group of the Śramaṇas came into being."

The *Aggañña Sutta*, as will be clear from the above two passages, distinguishes between Brahmin ascetics and Śramaṇas. It adds that a Brahmin can become a Śramaṇa, which implies that two ways of asceticism are open to the Brahmin. The properly Brahmanic way is characterized by a leaf hut in the jungle. The Śramaṇa, as against this, is stated to "go forth into the homeless life" (*anagāriyaṃ pabbajati*). The other features attributed to the Brahmin ascetic – being without fire, begging for food in villages and towns – are puzzling and do not agree well with the other sources of information which we have considered so far.

A more detailed description of a Brahmin ascetic contained in the Buddhist canon shows that tending the fire did after all characterize at least some of them. I refer to the matted hair ascetic (*jaṭila*) Kāśyapa of Uruvilvā, whose encounter with the Buddha is described in the *Mahāvagga* of the *Vinaya Piṭaka*.[6] [79]

5. DN III p. 95 f.: *ahu kho so vāseṭṭha samayo yaṃ khattiyo pi sakaṃ dhammaṃ garahamāno agārasmā anagāriyaṃ pabbajati 'samaṇo bhavissāmīti' / brāhmaṇo pi sakaṃ dhammaṃ garahamāno agārasmā anagāriyaṃ pabbajati 'samaṇo bhavissāmīti' / vesso pi sakaṃ dhammaṃ garahamāno agārasmā anagāriyaṃ pabbajati 'samaṇo bhavissāmīti' / suddo pi sakaṃ dhammaṃ garahamāno agārasmā anagāriyaṃ pabbajati 'samaṇo bhavissāmīti' / imehi kho vāseṭṭha catūhi maṇḍalehi samaṇamaṇḍalassa abhinibatti ahosi /*. Tr. RHYS DAVIDS, 1921: 92, modified.

6. Vin I p. 24 f., also CPS ch. 24; for a comparison with the two Chinese parallels, see BAREAU, 1963: 257-266.

Kāśyapa is not only a Brahmin (Vin I p. 25), but he is clearly presented as a Vedic ascetic who tends the sacred fire, for he lives in an *āśrama*, where he has a fire-house (*agyāgāra*, *aggisālā*). It is in this fire-house that the Buddha is going to combat a mighty snake, which represents no doubt Kāśyapa's power. No need to add, the Buddha subdues the snake, or more precisely, he destroys with his fire the fire of the snake. Kāśyapa is subsequently converted,[7] which may safely be interpreted to mean that he accepts the Buddha's powers to be greater than his own.

Another matted hair ascetic (*jaṭila*) is Keṇiya, who figures in the *Sela Sutta* (Sn p. 102 (99) ff.; MN II p. 146) and in the *Mahāvagga* of the *Vinaya Piṭaka* (Vin I p. 245 f.). Keṇiya, too, lives in an *āśrama*, and is described as "favourably disposed to the Brahmins" (*brāhmaṇesu abhippasanno*).

The Buddhist scriptures mention numerous encounters between the Buddha and one or several Brahmins. In the majority of cases the Brahmins concerned are not ascetics.[8] The *Subha Sutta* of the *Majjhima Nikāya* does however mention asceticism (*tapa*) as a Brahmanic virtue, along with truth, chastity (*brahmacariya*), study, and renunciation (*cāga*).[9] These same terms – in
[80] Sanskrit *satya*, *brahmacarya*, *adhyayana* and *tyāga* respectively – occur frequently in combination with tapas in the MBh to describe Brahmanic virtues.[10]

There can be no doubt that the Buddhist texts do at times use the term Brahmin in order to refer to Brahmin ascetics. A clear example is SN IV p. 118:[11] "Fasting, sleeping on the ground,

7. In the original account perhaps immediately after this event; see BAREAU, 1963: 261-62.
8. This led THOMAS (1933: 86) to the conclusion that "[t]he brahmins are never referred to as living an ascetic life". We have seen, and will see below, that this is not correct.
9. MN II p. 199.
10. See HARA, 1979: 29 ff.
11. SN IV p. 118 (read with the emendations proposed in WOODWARD,

bathing early in the morning and [reciting] the three Vedas, [wearing] rough hides, with matted hair and dirt, [uttering] sacred syllables, following ethical rules and observances, using ascetic practices, hypocrisy, deceit, sticks, the various ritual uses of water, *these are the characteristics of the Brahmins*, practised for some insignificant gain." This happens however almost exclusively in combination with the term Śramaṇa, even where clearly only Brahmins are intended. Consider, for example, the *Ambaṭṭha Sutta* of the *Dīgha Nikāya*. Here the Buddha enumerates (DN I p. 101) four 'gates of destruction' (*apāyamukha*) which a Śramaṇa or Brahmin may, unwisely, choose instead of the highest attainment of wisdom and conduct (*anuttarā vijjācaraṇasampadā*). The third of these 'gates' is of particular interest: it concerns the 'Śramaṇa or Brahmin' who erects a fire-house (*agyāgāra*) near a village or small town and stays there looking after (*paricaranto*) the fire. There can be no doubt that the fire talked about is the Vedic fire, and that the 'Śramaṇa or Brahmin' is a Brahmin. This is again confirmed by the fact that the description of this third gate occurs in a discussion with Ambaṭṭha, a Brahmin who takes pride in his descent.

However, the third 'gate of destruction' must be read along [81]
with the other three. The first concerns the 'Śramaṇa or Brahmin' who lives on fruits that have fallen of themselves,[12] the second concerns the 'Śramaṇa or Brahmin' who only eats bulbs, roots and fruits,[13] and the fourth concerns one who entertains passing Śramaṇas and Brahmins. These four 'gates of destruction' together combine many of the features that we find in the Brahmanic ascetic studied in earlier chapters. Their mention in a

---

1927: 75 n. 2, 5): *anāsakā thaṇḍilasāyikā ca / pātosinānañ ca tayo ca vedā // kharājinaṃ jaṭāpaṅko / mantā sīlabbataṃ tapo // kuhanā vaṅkaṃ daṇḍā ca / udakā ca majjāni* (?) *ca // vaṇṇā ete brāhmaṇānaṃ / katā kiñcikkhabhāvanā //*. Tr. KLOPPENBORG, 1990: 56.

12. *pavattaphalabhojana*. Cf. chapter 1 n. 11, above.

13. *kandamūlaphalabhojana*

discussion with a pretentious Brahmin appears to indicate that indeed all the characteristics of the four 'gates' were actually practised by Brahmin ascetics.

Theragāthā 219-221 describes the conversion to the Buddha's method by someone who used to tend the (sacrificial) fire in the forest (*aggiṃ paricariṃ vane*) and practised asceticism (*akāsiṃ ... tapaṃ*; 219), who used to be a kinsman of Brahmā, but has now become a true Brahmin (*brahmabandhu pure āsiṃ, idāni kho 'mhi brāhmaṇo*; 221).

The testimony of Megasthenes (chapter 1, above) gave the impression that Śramaṇas and Brahmins were different groups altogether. The Śramaṇas corresponded to what we call the non-Vedic ascetics, the Brahmins encompassed the Vedic ascetics. The passages studied above, on the other hand, seem to mix up the two terms. This kind of confusion is not exceptional in the Buddhist texts. The *Cūḷaassapura Sutta* of the *Majjhima Nikāya* (no. 40) lists quite a number of Śramaṇas whose Śramaṇa-ship (*sāmañña*) is stated not to depend exclusively on this or that feature (MN I p. 281-82). We read here, for example, that the Śramaṇa-ship of one who is unclothed (*acelaka*) does not
[82] depend on his being unclothed, and other similar cases which are not problematic. The same list, however, speaks also of "one who bathes ceremonially" (*udakorohaka*), "one who meditates on chants" (*mantajjhāyaka*), and "one who has matted hair" (*jaṭilaka*). All of these are Brahmins. I.B. Horner (1954: 335 n. 2) draws attention to other text passages (SN IV p. 312 = AN V p. 263) which use the first expression to refer to Brahmins of the west. The other two expressions are clear by themselves. We see, then, that the expression *sāmañña* 'Śramaṇa-ship' can here be used in connection with a Brahmin.

It is to be noted that Brahmins are not infrequently associated with special powers in the Buddhist texts. In the discussion with Ambaṭṭha we learn first that his ancestor Kaṇha was not really a Brahmin. But Kaṇha became a great Ṛṣi by studying the sacred mantras (*brahme mante*; DN I p. 96). These gave him great powers, which protected him against an attempt by king Okkāko to kill him with an arrow.

We have not, so far, spoken of the Buddhist Jātakas. Yet these texts contain much valuable information about different kinds of ascetics, both in the original gāthās and in the later, but still old, prose commentary. Before we turn to the stories, some preliminary remarks must be made.

Jātakas recount what happened to the Buddha to be (Bodhisattva; Pāli Bodhisatta) during his earlier lives, i.e., before he had found the way to Nirvāṇa. We cannot therefore expect to find Buddhist ascetics in these stories. (An exception must be made for the occasional Pratyekabuddha/Paccekabuddha; these figures remain however marginal and imprecise.) We do find other kinds of asceticism, which find however varying degrees of favour in these stories. The reason is clear. The Bodhisattva [83]
being an ascetically inclined person, he is often presented as an ascetic in the Jātakas. But the form of asceticism which he practises is necessarily non- or only partially Buddhist, yet cannot be described by the Buddhist authors as totally worthless.

Consider the *Vessantara-Jātaka*. This Jātaka, the longest one, refers repeatedly to what we have called Vedic asceticism. The banished prince Vessantara is often referred as "looking like a Brahmin with his matted hair and garment of animal skin, with his hook and sacrificial ladle, sleeping on the ground and reverencing the sacred fire".[14] He lives, with wife and children, in a leaf-hut (*paṇṇasālā*) in the forest (*vana*), eating roots and fruit obtained by gathering.[15] Royal ascetics (*rājisi*) who have

14. Jā VI p. 528 gāthā 2011, p. 529 gāthā 2016, p. 530 gāthā 2034, p. 533 gāthā 2055, p. 534 gāthā 2059, p. 539 gāthā 2115: *dhārento brāhmaṇaṃ vaṇṇaṃ āsadañ camasañ jaṭaṃ / cammavāsī chamā seti jātavedaṃ namassati //*. Tr. CONE and GOMBRICH, 1977: 47, 48, 49, 52, 53.

15. Jā VI p. 51[illegible] gāthā 1923 (*[illegible]na*), p. 518 gāthā 1948 (*paṇṇasālā*), p. 542 gāthā 2121 (*atho uñchena yāpema, atho mūlaphalā bahū*).

offered in the sacred fire (*āhutaggi*) dwell in the same area.[16] A special mention is made of the seer (*isi*) Accuta, who lives in an *āśrama* (*assama*) and is described in exactly the same terms as Vessantara above.[17]

Other Jātakas, too, know the Vedic ascetic.[18] The Asātamanta-Jātaka, for example, concerns a Brahmin boy who, when he is sixteen, is told by his parents: "Son, having kindled fire on the day of your birth, we have kept it burning. If you desire to become one whose heart is set on the World of Brahman, take the fire, enter the forest, and set your heart on the World of
[84] Brahman, worshipping the Lord of Fire."[19] The boy is also offered the choice to become a householder. These two ways of life are here presented as alternatives, not as constituting a sequence.

Almost the same words are used by the parents of the Bodhisatta in the Naṅguṭṭha-Jātaka. Here, however, they add that if their son prefers to become a householder, he has to learn the three Vedas.[20] In other words, the Vedic ascetic does not necessarily know the Vedas according to this text![21]

Even more interesting is the end of the Naṅguṭṭha-Jātaka. Here the Bodhisatta, after an unpleasant experience, extinguishes the fire with water, departs to become an Ṛṣi, and becomes one

16. Jā VI p. 518 gāthā 1935.
17. Jā VI p. 532 gāthās 2037-38.
18. See MEHTA, 1937: 572-73.
19. Jā I p. 285: *putta, mayaṃ tāva jātadivase aggiṃ gahetvā ṭhapayimha, sace Brahmalokaparāyano bhavitukāmo taṃ aggiṃ ādāya araññaṃ pavisitvā Aggiṃ Bhagavantaṃ namassamāno Brahmalokaparāyano hohi ...*
20. Jā I p. 494: *mayan te putta jātadivase aggiṃ gaṇhimha, sace si agāraṃ ajjhāvasitukāmo tayo vede uggaṇha, atha Brahmalokaṃ gantukāmo aggiṃ gahetvā araññaṃ pavisitvā aggiṃ paricaranto Mahābrahmā-naṃ ārādhetvā Brahmalokaparāyano hohīti.*
21. The beginning of the *Sona-Nanda-Jātaka* (Jā V p. 312) suggests rather that the choice between married life and asceticism is made after the Vedas have been learned.

whose heart is set on the World of Brahman.[22] Here two forms of asceticism are contrasted with each other, the one Vedic, the other without sacred fire, and therefore non-Vedic. It is also clear that the author of this Jātaka prefers by far the non-Vedic version.

Something quite similar happens in the Santhava-Jātaka. Here too the Bodhisatta has to choose between learning the three Vedas and becoming a householder on the one hand, and tending the sacred fire in the forest on the other. He chooses the latter [85]
alternative, has an unpleasant experience, extinguishes his fire with water, beating (?) it with sticks, enters the ascetic state of an Ṛṣi, and reaches the World of Brahman.[23] It seems clear that the ascetic state of being an Ṛṣi (*isipabbajjā*) is here (unlike in the case of Accuta, see above) not characterized by tending the Vedic fire.

The Jātakas do not tell us much about the two types of non-Vedic ascetics which we have come to distinguish. Some do indeed live in *āśrama*s, feeding on roots and fruit which they find in the forest, while others go begging in towns and villages. But several Jātakas create the impression that the non-Vedic ascetics can move from one of these two life-styles to the other and back again for no clear reason. Consider the *Uddālaka-Jātaka*. Uddālaka, having been made the teacher of a group of ascetics, asks the latter: "Sirs, you always live in the forest, feeding on roots and fruit from the woods; why don't you go where there are people?" They reply: "Sir, the people give us gifts, then expect gratitude from us, want us to speak of the Dhamma, ask questions; for fear of this we don't go to them."[24] There is no doubt a fair amount of Buddhist irony in

22. Jā I p. 495: ... *Mahāsatto aggiṃ udakena nibbāpetvā isipabajjaṃ pabbajitvā ... Brahmalokaparāyano ahosi.*

23. Jā II p. 43-45.

24. Jā IV p. 298: *atha ne so āha: "mārisā tumhe niccaṃ vanamūlaphalā-hārā araññe yeva vasatha, manussapathaṃ kasmā na gacchathā" ti / "mārisa, manussā nāma dānaṃ datvā anumodanaṃ kārāpenti*

this account of the ascetics' reason to stay away from society. Indeed, the sequel of the story recounts how the ascetics at last follow Uddālaka to Benares, only to be exposed as knaves. One gains at the same time the impression that the composers of the Jātakas did not know very well why some non-Vedic ascetics remained in the forest, while others came to beg their food in
[86] towns and villages. This is all the more noticeable since, as we have seen, the difference between Vedic and non-Vedic ascetics had not escaped their attention.

We have seen (chapter 1) that the Jaina canon has a tendency to use the term *parivrājaka* to refer to Brahmins, thus confusing to some extent the original distinction between Śramaṇas and Brahmins. The distinction is nevertheless known, for the compound *samaṇamāhaṇa*, 'Śramaṇas and Brahmins', occurs in the *Sūyagaḍa*.[25] In an enumeration of five types of beggars (*vaṇīmaga*), moreover, Brahmins (*māhaṇa*) and Śramaṇas are mentioned separately.[26] It is not, however, certain that we must in this last case think of Brahmins who actually beg for their food; it is also conceivable that Brahmins in general are here described as potential recipients of gifts. The institution of Brahmin asceticism, on the other hand, is well known to the Jaina canon, as is shown by the references given at the end of chapter 1, above.

---

dhammakathaṃ kathāpenti pañhaṃ pucchanti, mayaṃ tena bhayena tattha na gacchāma"/

25. Sūy 2.2.696.
26. Ṭhāṇ 5.3.454; see JAIN, 1984: 316.

Chapter 11. Asceticism in the *Mahābhārata* [87]

The MBh does not appear to distinguish between Śramaṇas and Brahmins. The two kinds of ascetics that we are studying are, however, not unknown to this epic. But where the Buddhist and Jaina texts contain much information about non-Vedic asceticism, the MBh contains, in its narrative portions, mainly information about Vedic asceticism.

We have considered a number of Vedic ascetics from the MBh in chapter 6, above. Their asceticism takes place in connection with the Vedic sacrifice or replaces it. Its aims are by and large the same as those of the sacrifice: reaching heaven, preferably in bodily form, supporting the gods in their fights with the demons, obtaining certain powers, obtaining a son, etc.[1] Vedic asceticism can therefore be looked upon as an extension and elaboration of the ascetic elements which are present in the Vedic sacrifice.

Non-Vedic asceticism, as we have come to know it in the preceding pages, has quite different aims.[2] It aims primarily at

1. See SHEE, 1986: 346 f. Cf. HARA, 1979: 511 ff. On the connection that existed, and exists, between ascetics and other 'holy men' on the one hand, and performing magicians on the other, see SIEGEL, 1991: passim. On levitation, for example, SIEGEL observes (p. 215): "It's impossible to know if such religious stories ... result from people having seen magicians do the levitation trick, from their need to explain it, or if the trick is invented, its method worked out, by magicians who have heard the stories and realize that, because people believe such things as levitation are possible and a mark of merit or of ritual accomplishment, there is power to be had in the performance of them. In either case, the street magicians, of the present as well as of the past, try to elicit religious associations."
2. HARA (1979: 517) notices, with regard to the MBh, "the incapability of *tapas* to be ranked among the highest religious ideals (*vairāgya, mokṣa,*

[88] inaction, with the ultimate goal of liberation from the effects of one's actions. These are hardly ideals which easily give rise to stories, as do the aims of the Vedic ascetic. We may however be sure that where the two forms of asceticism confront each other, the non-Vedic ascetic can not really be expected to deny the powers which the Vedic ascetic claims to possess, or acquire; this would obviously weaken his position in the eyes of all outsiders. Rather one would expect to find passages where the non-Vedic ascetic is counseled against the use of these powers.

A confrontation of this type is found in the longer version of the story of Śamīka and Śṛṅgin.[3] WEZLER (1979) has argued that this is the amplified form of the shorter version,[4] and has itself suffered at least one addition. Whether or not this be the case, there are some important points to be noted. Both the long and the short version describe Śamīka as an ascetic characterized by motionlessness and silence, at least during the events which make up the story. He is "like a tree trunk" (*sthāṇubhūta*, 1.37.7; *sthāṇuvat*, 1.45.25) and "observing silence" (*maunavrate sthita*, 1.36.18, 46.7; *anabhibhāṣin*, 1.37.6; *maunavratadhara*, 1.45.25; etc.), even when king Parikṣit puts in anger a dead snake on his shoulder. In fact, he does nothing to remove the snake even after the departure of the king (*tathaiva āste*, 1.36.20, 37.9; etc.). The parallelism with certain stories from Jaina literature is striking,[5] and one is tempted to conclude that Śamīka's asceticism is of the non-Vedic type. This seems confirmed in the last part of the longer version, where Śamīka states unambiguously that the ascetic should abandon anger and
[89] cultivate serenity (*śama*) and forgiveness (*kṣamā*). The object of

---

nirvāṇa), which are never found in the accusative case in such passages where *tapas* stands in the instrumental."

3. MBh 1.36.8 – 1.38.26.

4. MBh 1.45.20 f.

5. See, e.g., Āyāraṅga 9.2, tr. JAINI, 1979: 26; further WEZLER, 1979: 55.

these instructions is Śamīka's son Śṛṅgin who had, in an attack of anger, directed his ascetic powers against king Parikṣit. It will be clear that those who follow Śamīka's advice are hardly the characters that could provide the MBh with its many stories about ascetics. Even Śamīka found his way into the epic owing to the fact that his son – also a great ascetic – was less restrained than his father.

This interpretation of the story of Śamīka and Śṛṅgin, however, can be no more than tentative, for two reasons. The first one is that the story does not tell us whether Śamīka is in search of liberation, the differentiating characteristic of the non-Vedic tradition. This means that we have to judge on the basis of his practices. But Vedic ascetic practices are frequently very similar to non-Vedic ones. The theme of motionlessness characterizes also ascetics who strive for more worldly aims. Cyavana Bhārgava, for example, remains 'like a tree trunk' (*sthāṇubhūta*; MBh 3.122.2) until an ant-hill has formed around him; he uses his ascetic powers to cause constipation in the army of the king, then marries his daughter. Sāvitrī stands upright 'as though she had become wood' (*kāṣṭhabhūteva*; MBh 3.280.8) in order to save her husband from death. The three Ṛṣis Ekata, Dvita and Trita stand on one leg for four thousand years 'like pieces of wood' (*kāṣṭhabhūta*; MBh 12.323.20) in order to see Nārāyaṇa.

Opposition against the use of the powers arising from asceticism is also found in the philosophic portions of the MBh. These portions frequently speak of Yoga, which is considered to give rise to supernatural powers. However, "he who having passed beyond the supernatural powers of Yoga, leaves them behind,
is released".[6] These powers are described as "mastery over [the [90]
gross elements] earth, air, ether, water, and fire, and of the I-faculty" (12.228.14) or "mastery of the unmanifest (*avyakta*)" (15). Elsewhere we read: "The Yoga-follower, having attained

6. MBh 12.228.37cd: *yogaiśvaryam atikrānto yo 'tikrāmati mucyate*. Here and in what follows I make use of EDGERTON's (1965) translation.

power, can create many thousands of selves (i.e., may make himself many-thousand fold), and may roam the earth in all these (guises)" (12.289.26).

The real aim of Yoga, in these passages, is different from these supernatural powers: "As an archer that is attentive and concentrated hits the target, so the perfectly disciplined (*yukta*) yogin attains liberation (*mokṣa*), without a doubt" (12.289.31). This same chapter of the MBh explains that Yoga consists in disciplining the self so that it is motionless (33), remaining motionless (38). Exercises in concentration (*samādhi*) and fixation (*dhāraṇā*) are obviously means to attain this aim.

There is no need to multiply citations, for the nature of epic Yoga is already well-known. Nor is it necessary to analyse the 'philosophies' presented in the MBh – often referred to as Sāṅkhya – which share the idea of a motionless self; they have to, because these 'philosophies' constitute the knowledge which is deemed to lead to liberation.[7]

We must address the question whether the two forms of asceticism which we have come to distinguish – Vedic and non-Vedic – are referred to by the two terms *tapas* and *yoga* respectively. A priori there is much that seems to support this. The literal meaning of *tapas* 'heat' fits well in the Vedic sacrificial context. *Yoga*, on the other hand, is frequently used in combination with Sāṃkhya; both terms refer to methods that lead to liberation.[8]

[91] It must not, however, be overlooked that both the terms *tapas* and *yoga* are used in connection with both Vedic and non-Vedic asceticism. We have also seen that supernatural powers are ascribed to the practice of *Yoga*. All this can, of course, be easily explained on the assumption that the two forms of asceticism influenced each other and borrowed each other's terminology. This may very well be the correct explanation, yet

7. See EDGERTON, 1965: 35 f.; BRONKHORST, 1986: 51 f.

8. See HARA, 1979: 517, cited in n. 2 above; and HOPKINS, 1901: 367 f.

I know of no evidence which would definitely prove the original dichotomy between *tapas* and *yoga*. Their original connection with only Vedic and non-Vedic asceticism respectively remains therefore an attractive, but unproven, hypothesis.

To conclude this chapter I would like to draw attention to an episode in the MBh where explicit Vedic elements appear to have been added to a story which was originally without them; this is the episode of Duḥṣanta and Śakuntalā (1.64 f.). Duḥṣanta chances upon the hermitage where Śakuntalā lives. He sees Brahmins engaged in Vedic rites (1.64.16-17, 30, 38, 40) and hears the sound of Vedic recitation (20-22, 31). In spite of this, he then discovers that the hermitage is empty, and shouts: "Who is here?" (*ka iha*; 1.65.2). The preceding description of numerous men engaged in Vedic rites and recitation appears to be an addition to the story, for the Vedic element does not recur in it.[9]

9. On the origin of the Epic Śakuntalā story, see INSLER, 1991, esp. p. 123 f.

Part IV

General conclusions

Chapter 12. Concluding observations [92]

The preceding chapters have shown that early India knew ascetic practices in two different religious contexts. On the one hand there were the non-Vedic religious currents which encompassed, and gave rise to, Jainism and other 'śramaṇic' beliefs and practices, and which shared a conviction in rebirth as a result of one's actions, and sought ways to stop this. On the other hand there was Vedic religion which, for reasons of its own, required ascetic restrictions in connection with the execution of the sacrifice. The non-Vedic search for liberation occasioned the presence of life-long ascetics and wanderers more or less as a matter of course. The Vedic restrictions, normally confined to the duration of a sacrifice, inspired some to make of them a way of life, and were in any case believed to lead the practitioner to the same aims as those which others tried to reach by performing sacrifices. This led to the existence, side by side, of essentially two different types of ascetics in ancient India, often called Śramaṇas and Brahmins respectively. Both among the Śramaṇas and among the Brahmins a further twofold distinction can be observed. Early sources, including Megasthenes, confirm these distinctions. The differences between the two main groups of ascetics were more than superficial; they concerned their aims, and consequently also their behaviour.

No doubt aided by popular opinion, which could not always distinguish between the two, both kinds of asceticism became
more and more blurred, and characteristics of the one came to be [93]
ascribed to the other, and vice versa. The final result of this process is the classical doctrine of the four *āśrama*s, in which all distinctions have become blended, or rather added on to each other. If we had no other evidence than this classical doctrine to

go by, the double origin of Indian asceticism would remain hidden from us.

Which is the exact position of Buddhism within the scheme elaborated in the preceding pages? Buddhism plays virtually no role in the present book. Buddhist texts were used, to be sure, but only in order to obtain information about non-Buddhist ascetics, primarily Brahmins. Buddhism could be left out precisely because it plays practically no role in the developments here studied. It is of course clear that early Buddhism had links with non-Vedic asceticism. Indeed, the Buddha himself is frequently referred to as a Śramaṇa. But early Buddhism distinguished itself clearly from the other forms of non-Vedic asceticism, and its aims and methods should not be confused with the latter. Some authors believe that what seem to be distinctive features of early Buddhism must be reinterpreted so as to agree better with what we know of the other religions of its day.[1] This approach, which tells the texts what they should contain, rather than trying to find out what they actually have to say, must of course be discarded as unacceptable.

It seems, then, that early Buddhism, in spite of the efforts of
[94] some modern scholars to obfuscate this, was in fact markedly different from the other religious movements that existed in its day. It shared, to be sure, many of the ideas (rebirth determined by one's actions) and ideals (reaching freedom from rebirth) with the non-Vedic current which we have identified, yet appears to have introduced an altogether different method to reach this goal. Earliest Buddhism as we know it from the texts does not preach immobility of body and mind, nor does it search

1. See, e.g., Paul MUS's (1935: I: *41) remark: "Mais alors le bouddhisme initial se trouvant séparé des superstitions populaires et des pratiques cultuelles les plus actives à l'époque où il fut formulé, et les acquisitions successives étant réputées hétérogènes, l'histoire de cette religion ne sera plus constituée que d'exceptions et de renoncements." MUS offers, of course, a way 'pour échapper à ces anomalies'.

for the true, i.e. inactive, nature of the soul. It is true that Buddhism, which thus took a direction of its own, soon came to adopt certain practices which it had initially abandoned. And typically Buddhist practices found their way back into the non-Buddhist movements, thus contributing to the checkered image of asceticism in classical India. Since these developments and mutual influences have been studied elsewhere,[2] they will not be discussed in further detail here.

By way of conclusion it may be useful to emphasize once more that the description of Indian asceticism in its historical development presented in this book is, and can be, no more than a broad outline of this development. It would be a truism to add that the historical reality that hides behind the scheme presented was without a shadow of a doubt richer and more varied than this description may suggest. This does not, however, detract from whatever value it may have. Broad outlines have their use, and, if correct, can constitute major advances in our understanding. We all know that the earth is no sphere; yet the discovery that the earth is almost spherical was, in its time, a significant step ahead. Insisting that the shape of the earth is too complicated to describe cannot compare to it in informative value.

2. see BRONKHORST, 1986. (Added in the 2nd edition:) See also the Preface to the second edition of that book, and BRONKHORST, 1995.

Bibliography

Ahirbudhnya Saṃhitā. Edited by Pt. M.D. Ramanujacharya, under the supervision of F. Otto Schrader; revised by Pt. V. Krishnamacharya. 2 vols. Madras: The Adyar Library and Research Centre. Second edition 1966. (Adyar Library Series, 4.)

Āpastamba Dharma Sūtra. Āpastambīyadharmasūtram, edited by George Bühler. Third edition. Poona: Bhandarkar O.R. Institute. 1932. (Bombay Sanskrit Series, 44 and 50.)

Arthaśāstra. The Kauṭilīya Arthaśāstra. Part I: edition; part II: translation; part III: study. By R.P. Kangle. Reprint. Delhi: Motilal Banarsidass. 1986.

Āruṇi Upaniṣad = Schrader, 1912: 3-12.

Aśvaghoṣa: *Buddhacarita*. Edited and translated by E.H. Johnston. Reprint: Delhi: Motilal Banarsidass. 1978.

Bakker, Hans (1989): *De Leer van de Wind. Een natuurfilosofie uit de Upanisaden*. Ingeleid, vertaald en geannoteerd. Kampen: Kok Agora.

Bareau, André (1963): *Recherches sur la biographie du Buddha dans les Sūtrapiṭaka et les Vinayapiṭaka anciens: de la quête de l'éveil à la conversion de Śāriputra et de Maudgalyāyana*. Paris: École Française d'Extrême-Orient. (Publications de l'EFEO, 53.)

Basham, A.L. (1989): *The Origins and Development of Classical Hinduism*. Edited and annotated by Kenneth G. Zysk. Boston: Beacon Press.

Baudhāyana Dharma Sūtra. The Baudhāyanadharmaśāstra, edited by E. Hultzsch. Leipzig 1884. Genehmigter Nachdruck: Kraus Reprint, Nendeln, Liechtenstein. 1966. (Abhandlungen für die Kunde des Morgenlandes, VIII. Band, No. 4.)

Bedekar, V.M. (1964): "The place of japa in the Mokṣadharmaparvan (MB. [96]
XII 189-193) and the Yoga-Sūtras: a comparative study." *Annals of the Bhandarkar Oriental Research Institute* 44 (1963), 63-74.

Biardeau, Madeleine (1964): *Théorie de la connaissance et philosophie de la parole dans le brahmanisme classique*. Paris – La Haye: Mouton.

Biardeau, Madeleine (1976): "Le sacrifice dans l'hindouisme." In: *Le sacrifice dans l'Inde ancienne*, by Madeleine Biardeau and Charles Malamoud. Paris: Presses Universitaires de France. (Bibliothèque de l'École des Hautes Études, Section des Sciences Religieuses, Vol. LXXIX.) Pp. 7-154.

Biardeau, Madeleine (1981): *L'hindouisme. Anthropologie d'une civilisation.* Paris: Flammarion.

Bock, Andreas (1984): *Der Sāgara-Gaṅgāvatarana-Mythus in der episch -purāṇischen Literatur.* Stuttgart: Franz Steiner. (Alt- und Neu-Indische Studien, 27.)

Bodewitz, H.W. (1973): *Jaiminīya Brāhmaṇa* I, 1-65. Translation and commentary, with a study Agnihotra and Prāṇāgnihotra. Leiden: Brill.

Böhtlingk, Otto (1889): *Khândogjopanishad.* Kritisch herausgegeben und übersetzt. Leipzig: H. Haessel.

Boyer, A.-M. (1901): "Étude sur l'origine de la doctrine du saṃsāra." *Journal Asiatique*, Neuvième Série, 18, pp. 451-499.

Bṛhadāraṇyaka Upaniṣad = Limaye and Vadekar, 1958: 174-282.

Brockington, J. L. (1981): *The Sacred Thread. Hinduism in its continuity and diversity.* Edinburgh University Press. 1989.

Bronkhorst, Johannes (1983): "God in Sāṃkhya." *Wiener Zeitschrift für die Kunde Südasiens* 27, 149-164.

Bronkhorst, Johannes (1985): "Patañjali and the Yoga sūtras." *Studien zur Indologie und Iranistik* 10 (1984), 191-212.

[97] Bronkhorst, Johannes (1986): *The Two Traditions of Meditation in Ancient India.* Stuttgart: Franz Steiner Verlag Wiesbaden. (Alt- und Neu-Indische Studien, 28.) A new edition has been published by Motilal Banarsidass, Delhi, 1993.

Bronkhorst, Johannes (1989): "L'indianisme et les préjugés occidentaux." *Études de Lettres* (Revue de la Faculté des Lettres, Université de Lausanne) 1989, 2, 119-136.

Bronkhorst, Johannes (1991): "Pāṇini and the nominal sentence." *Annals of the Bhandarkar Oriental Research Institute* 71 (1990), 301-304.

Bronkhorst, Johannes (1995): "The Buddha and the Jainas reconsidered." *Asiatische Studien / Études Asiatiques* 49(2), 333-350.

Bühler, Georg (tr.)(1879): *The Sacred Laws of the Āryas as Taught in the Schools of Āpastamba, Gautama, Vasishṭha and Baudhāyana.* Part I: Āpastamba and Gautama. Delhi: Motilal Banarsidass. 1986. (Sacred Books of the East, 2.)

Bühler, Georg (tr.)(1882): *The Sacred Laws of the Āryas as Taught in the Schools of Āpastamba, Gautama, Vāsishtha and Baudhāyana.* Part II: Vāsishtha and Baudhāyana. Delhi: Motilal Banarsidass. 1984. (Sacred Books of the East, 14.)

Burkert, Walter (1985): *Greek Religion. Archaic and Classical.* Translated by John Raffan. Oxford: Basil Blackwell. 1990.

Butzenberger, Klaus (1996): "Ancient Indian conceptions on man's destiny after death. The beginnings and the early development of the doctrine of transmigration. I." *Berliner Indologische Studien* 9, 55-118.

Caland, W. (tr.)(1929): *Vaikhānasasmārtasūtram. The domestic rules and sacred laws of the Vaikhānasa school belonging to the Black Yajurveda.* Calcutta: Asiatic Society of Bengal.

Caland, W., and Henry, V. (1906-07): *L'Agniṣṭoma: Description complète de la forme normale du sacrifice de soma dans le culte védique.* 2 tomes. Paris: Ernest Leroux.

Catuṣpariṣat Sūtra. 1) Edition: *Das Catuṣpariṣatsūtra, eine kanonische Lehrschrift über die Begründung der buddhistischen Gemeinde.* Text in Sanskrit und Tibetisch, verglichen mit dem Pāli nebst einer Übersetzung der chinesischen Entsprechung im Vinaya der MūlaSarvāstivādins. Auf Grund von Turfān-Handschriften herausgegeben und bearbeitet von Ernst WaldSchmidt. Teil II. Textbearbeitung. Berlin 1962.
(Abhandlungen der deutschen Akademie der Wissenschaften zu Berlin. [98]
Klasse für Sprachen, Literatur und Kunst, Jahrgang 1960, Nr. 1.) 2) Translation: *The Sūtra on the Foundation of the Buddhist Order*, translated by Ria Kloppenborg. Leiden: E.J. Brill. 1973.

Chāndogya Upaniṣad = Limaye and Vadekar, 1958: 68-173

Chandra, Pratap (1971): "Was early Buddhism influenced by the Upaniṣads?" *Philosophy East and West* 21, 317-324.

Collins, Steven (1982): *Selfless Persons. Imagery and thought in Theravāda Buddhism.* Cambridge University Press.

Cone, Margaret, and Gombrich, Richard F. (1977): *The Perfect Generosity of Prince Vessantara: a Buddhist epic.* Oxford University Press.

Deleu, Jozef (1966): "Nirayāvaliyāsuyakkhandha – Uvanga's 8-12 van de jaina Canon." *Orientalia Gandensia* 3, 77-150. An English translation by J.W. de Jong and Royce Wiles has now been published: *Nirayāvali-yāsuyakkhandha: Uvanga's 8-12 of the Jain Canon*. Tokyo: The Chūō Academic Research Institute. 1996. (Philologica Asiatica, Monograph Series 10.)

Deleu, Jozef (1970): *Viyāhapannatti (Bhagavaī). The Fifth Anga of the Jaina Canon*. Introduction, critical analysis, commentary & indexes. Brugge: De Tempel.

Deshpande, Madhav M. (1990): "Changing conceptions of the Veda: from speech-acts to magical sounds." *Adyar Library Bulletin* 54, 1-41.

Deussen, Paul (tr.)(1887): *Die Sūtra's des Vedānta*. Leipzig: F.A. Brockhaus. Reprint Georg Olms Verlag, Hildesheim – New York, 1982.

Deussen, Paul (1906): *The Philosophy of the Upanishads*. Authorized English translation by A. S. Geden. New York: Dover. 1966.

Deussen, Paul (1909): "Āśrama." In: *Encyclopedia of Religion and Ethics* II (ed. James Hastings). Edinburgh: T. & T. Clark. Pp. 128-131.

Doniger, Wendy, with Smith, Brian K. (1991): *The Laws of Manu*. Penguin Books.

During Caspers, E.C.L. (1985): "Magic hunting practices in Harappan times." *South Asian Archaeology* 1985 (Denmark), 227-236.

[99] Dutt, Sukumar (1924): *Early Buddhist Monachism* (600 B.C. – 100 B.C.). London: Kegan Paul.

Edgerton, Franklin (1929): "The Upaniṣads: what do they seek, and why?" *Journal of the American Oriental Society* 49, 97-121.

Edgerton, Franklin (1965): *The Beginnings of Indian Philosophy. Selections from the Rig Veda, Atharva Veda, Upaniṣads, and Mahābhārata*, translated from the Sanskrit with an introduction, notes and glossarial index. London: George Allen & Unwin.

Eggeling, Julius (tr.)(1882-1900): *The Śatapatha-Brāhmaṇa, according to the Text of the Mādhyandina School*. Five volumes. Reprint. Delhi-Patna-Varanasi: Motilal Banasidass. 1966. (Sacred Books of the East, vol. XII, XXVI, XLI, XLIII, XLIV.)

Eggers, Wilhelm (1929): *Das Dharmasūtra der Vaikhānasas*. Nebst einer Einleitung über den brahmanischen Waldeinsiedler-Orden und die Vaikhānasa-Sekte. Göttingen: Vandenhoeck & Ruprecht.

Eliade, Mircea (1969): *Yoga: Immortality and Freedom*. Translated from the French by Willard R. Trask. Second Edition. Princeton University Press.

Falk, Harry (1986): *Bruderschaft und Würfelspiel. Untersuchungen zur Entwicklungsgeschichte des vedischen Opfers*. Freiburg: Hedwig Falk.

Farquhar, J.N. (1920): *An Outline of the Religious Literature of India*. Reprint. Delhi: Motilal Banarsidass. 1967.

Fausbøll, V. (ed.)(1877-1896): *The Jātaka*, together with its Commentary. 6 vols. Reprint: London: Pali Text Society. 1962-1964.

Filliozat, Jean (1937): *Étude de démonologie indienne*. Le Kumāratantra de Rāvaṇa, et les textes parallèles indiens, tibétains, chinois, cambodgiens et arabes. Paris: Imprimerie Nationale. (Cahiers de la Société Asiatique, Première Série, IV.)

Fleet, John Faithfull (1970): *Corpus Inscriptionum Indicarum*, vol III: [100]
Inscriptions of the early Gupta kings and their successors. Third revised edition. Varanasi: Indological Book House.

Forsyth, Neil (1987): *The Old Enemy. Satan and the combat myth*. Princeton University Press. Princeton Paperback. 1989.

Franke, R. Otto (tr.)(1913): *Dīghanikāya*. Das Buch der langen Texte des buddhistischen Kanons in Auswahl übersetzt. Göttingen: Vandenhoeck & Ruprecht.

Frauwallner, Erich (1953): *Geschichte der indischen Philosophie*. I. Band. Salzburg: Otto Müller.

Gampert, Wilhelm (1939): *Die Sühnezeremonien in der altindischen Rechtsliteratur*. Prag: Orientalisches Institut. (Monografie Archivu Orientálního, 6.)

Garbe, Richard (1903): "Die Weisheit des Brahmanen oder des Kriegers?" In: *Beiträge zur indischen Kulturgeschichte*. Berlin: Paetel. Pp. 1-36.

Gautama Dharma Sūtra. *Gautamapraṇītadharmasūtrāṇi*, edited, with Haradatta's *Mitākṣarā*, by Narahari Taḷekara. Poona: Ānandāśrama. 1959. (Ānandāśramasaṃskṛtagranthāvali, 61.)

Gombrich, Richard (1992): "The Buddha's book of Genesis?" *Indo-Iranian Journal* 35, 159-178.

Gonda, J. (1965): *Change and Continuity in Indian Religion*. The Hague: Mouton.

Gonda, Jan (1977): *The Ritual Sūtras*. Wiesbaden: Otto Harrassowitz. (A History of Indian Literature I, 2.)

Goudriaan, T. (1977): "Kaḍga-Rāvaṇa and his worship in Balinese and Indian Tantric sources." *Wiener Zeitschrift für die Kunde Südasiens* 21, 143-169.

Goudriaan, Teun (1981): "Hindu Tantric Literature in Sanskrit." = Goudriaan and Gupta, 1981: 1-172.

[101] Goudriaan, Teun, and Gupta, Sanjukta (1981): *Hindu Tantric and Śākta Literature*. Wiesbaden: Otto Harrassowitz. (A History of Indian Literature II, 2.)

Haberlandt, Michael (1885): "Ueber den dritten âçrama der Inder." *Mittheilungen der Anthropologischen Gesellschaft in Wien* 15 (N.F. 5), [10]-[12].

Hacker, Paul (1959): *Prahlāda. Werden und Wandel einer Idealgestalt.* Teil I. Wiesbaden: Franz Steiner. (Akademie der Wissenschaften und der Literatur. Abhandlungen der Geistes- und Sozialwissenschaftlichen Klasse. Jhrg. 1959, Nr. 9.)

Hacker, Paul (1978): "'Topos' und chrêsis. Ein Beitrag zum Gedankenaustausch zwischen den Geisteswissenschaften." *Kleine Schriften*, ed. by Lambert Schmithausen. Wiesbaden. Pp. 338-359.

Halbfass, Wilhelm (1991a): *Tradition and Reflection. Explorations in Indian thought.* State University of New York Press.

Halbfass, Wilhelm (1991b): "Early Indian references to the Greeks and the first Western references to Buddhism." In: *The Dating of the Historical Buddha / Die Datierung des historischen Buddha*. Part I. Ed. Heinz Bechert. Göttingen: Vandenhoeck & Ruprecht. Pp. 197-208.

Hara, Minoru (1975): "Indra and tapas." *Adyar Library Bulletin* 39, 129-160.

Hara, Minoru (1979): *Koten Indo no Kugyō* (Asceticism in Classical India). Tokyo.

Harvey, Peter (1990): *An Introduction to Buddhism.* Teachings, history and practices. Cambridge University Press.

Hauer, J.W. (1922): *Die Anfänge der Yogapraxis im alten Indien.* Stuttgart: W. Kohlhammer.

Heesterman, J.C. (1964): "Brahmin, ritual, and renouncer." *Wiener Zeitschrift für die Kunde Süd- und Ostasiens* 8, 1-31. Repr.: Heesterman, 1985: 26-44.

[102] Heesterman, J.C. (1982): "Householder and wanderer." In: *Way of Life. King, Householder, Renouncer.* Essays in honour of Louis Dumont. Edited by T.N. Madan. Paris: Éditions de la Maison des Sciences de l'Homme.

Heesterman, J.C. (1985): *The Inner Conflict of Tradition. Essays in Indian ritual, kingship, and society*. University of Chicago Press.

Hinüber, Oskar v. (1989): *Der Beginn der Schrift und frühe Schriftlichkeit in Indien*. Stuttgart: Franz Steiner. (Akademie der Wissenschaften und der Literatur, Abhandlungen der Geistes- und Sozialwissenschaftlichen Klasse, Jhrg. 1989 Nr. 11.)

Hinüber, Oskar v. (1991): "Linguistic considerations on the date of the Buddha." In: *The Dating of the Historical Buddha / Die Datierung des historischen Buddha*. Part I. Ed. Heinz Bechert. Göttingen: Vandenhoeck & Ruprecht. Pp. 183-193.

Hopkins, E. Washburn (1901): "Yoga-technique in the great epic." *Journal of the American Oriental Society* 22, 333-379.

Horner, I.B. (tr.)(1954): *The Middle Length Sayings* (Majjhima-Nikāya) Vol. I. London: Routledge & Kegan Paul. (Pali Text Society Translation Series, No. 29.) Second impression 1976.

Horsch, Paul (1966): *Die vedische Gāthā- und Śloka-Literatur*. Bern: Francke Verlag.

Horsch, Paul (1971): "Vorstufen der indischen Seelenwanderungslehre." *Asiatische Studien / Études Asiatiques* 25, 99-157.

Hume, Robert Ernest (tr.)(1931): *The Thirteen Principal Upanishads*. Second edition, revised. Oxford University Press. 1975.

Insler, Stanley (1991): "The shattered head split and the Epic tale of Śakuntalā." *Bulletin d'Études Indiennes* 7-8 (1989-1990), 97-139.

Jābāla Upaniṣad = Schrader, 1912: 59-72.

Jacobi, Hermann (tr.)(1884): *Jaina Sūtras*. Part I: The Ācārāṅga Sūtra, the Kalpa Sūtra. Delhi: Motilal Banarsidass. 1980. (Sacred Books of the East, vol. 22.)

Jain, J.Ch. (1984): *Life in Ancient India as Depicted in the Jain Canon and* [103]
Commentaries: 6th century BC to 17th century AD. Second rev. and enl. edition. New Delhi: Munshiram Manoharlal.

Jaini, P.S. (1970): "Śramaṇas: their conflict with brāhmaṇical society." In: *Chapters in Indian Civilisation*, Vol. I. Edited by Joseph W. Elder. Dubuque (Iowa): Kendall Hunt. Pp. 41-81.

Jaini, Padmanabh S. (1979): *The Jaina Path of Purification*. Delhi: Motilal Banarsidass.

Jha, Ganganatha (tr.)(1933): *Śābara-Bhāṣya*. 3 vol. Baroda: Oriental Institute. 1973-74.

Kaelber, Walter O. (1989): *Tapta Mārga. Asceticism and initiation in Vedic India*. State University of New York Press.

Kane, Pandurang Vaman: *History of Dharmaśāstra*. Vol. I, revised and enlarged, part 1, 1968; part 2, 1975. Vol. II, second edition, 2 parts, 1974. Vol. III, second edition, 1973. Vol. IV, second edition, 1973. Vol. V, second edition, part 1, 1974; part 2, 1977. Poona: Bhandarkar Oriental Research Institute.

Kangle, R.P. (1986): *The Kauṭilīya Arthaśāstra*. 3 parts. See under *Artha-śāstra*.

Karttunen, Klaus (1989): *India in Early Greek Literature*. Helsinki: Finnish Oriental Society. (Studia Orientalia, 65.)

Kaṭhaśruti = Schrader, 1912: 31-42.

Kaṭha Upaniṣad = Limaye and Vadekar, 1958: 11-27.

Keith, Arthur Berriedale (1925): *The Religion and Philosophy of the Veda and Upanishads*. 2 volumes. Second Indian reprint. Delhi: Motilal Banarsidass. 1976.

Kern, H. (1896): *Manual of Indian Buddhism*. Reprint. Varanasi - Delhi: Indological Book House. 1972.

Kloppenborg, Ria (1990): "The Buddha's redefinition of tapas (ascetic practice)." *Buddhist Studies Review* 7, 49-73.

[104] Knipe, David M. (1975): *In the Image of Fire. Vedic experiences of heat*. Delhi: Motilal Banarsidass.

Lalwani, K.C. (1985): *Bhagavatī Sūtra*. Vol. IV (Śatakas 9-11). Prakrit text with English translation. Calcutta: Jain Bhawan.

Lamotte, Étienne (1958): *Histoire du bouddhisme indien, des origines à l'ère Śaka*. Réimpr. 1967. Louvain: Institut Orientaliste. (Bibliothèque du Muséon, 43.)

Leumann, Ernst (1883): *Das Aupapātika Sūtra, erstes Upānga der Jaina*. I. Theil. Einleitung, Text und Glossar. Nachdruck: Kraus Reprint, Nendeln, Liechtenstein. 1966.

Lévi, Sylvain (1898): *La doctrine du sacrifice dans les Brāhmaṇas*. Paris: Ernest Leroux.

Limaye, V.P., and Vadekar, R.D. (ed.)(1958): *Eighteen Principal Upaniṣads*. Vol. I. (Upaniṣadic Text with Parallels from extant Vedic Literature, Exegetical and Grammatical Notes.) Poona: Vaidika Saṃśodhana Maṇḍala.

Lindner, Bruno (1878): *Die Dīkshā, oder Weihe für das Somaopfer*. Leipzig: Pöschel & Trepte.

Lingat, Robert (1967): *Les sources du droit dans le système traditionnel de l'Inde*. Paris – La Haye: Mouton.

Malamoud, Charles (1976): "Terminer le sacrifice." In: *Le sacrifice dans l'Inde ancienne*, by Madeleine Biardeau and Charles Malamoud. Paris: Presses Universitaires de France. (Bibliothèque de l'École des Hautes Études, Section des Sciences Religieuses, Vol. LXXIX.) Pp. 155-204.

Malamoud, Charles (1977): *Le svādhyāya, récitation personnelle du Veda. Taittirīya-Āraṇyaka II. Texte traduit et commenté*. Paris: E. de Boccard. (Publications de l'Institut de Civilisation Indiennes, 42.)

Malamoud, Charles (1989): *Cuire le monde: rite et pensée dans l'Inde ancienne*. Paris: Éditions la Découverte.

Mānava Śrauta Sūtra. Edited by Jeannette M. van Gelder. Reprint: Sri [105]
Satguru Publications, Delhi. 1985.

Marshall, John, et al. (1931): *Mohenjo-daro and the Indus Culture*. London. 3 vols.

McEvilley, Thomas (1981): "An archaeology of yoga." RES 1, 44-77.

McCrindle, J.W. (1877): *Ancient India as described by Megasthenes and Arrian*. Reprinted in: *McCrindle's Ancient India*, edited by Ramchandra Jain. New Delhi: Today & Tomorrow's Printers & Publishers. 1972.

Mehta, Ratilal (1937): "Asceticism in pre-Buddhist days." *Indian Culture* 3, 571-584.

Meisig, Konrad (1988): *Das Sūtra von den vier Ständen. Das Agañña-Sutta im Licht seiner chinesischen Parallelen*. Wiesbaden: Otto Harrassowitz. (Freiburger Beiträge zur Indologie, 20.)

Mesquita, R. (1991): Review of Nakamura, 1983. *Wiener Zeitschrift für die Kunde Südasiens* 35, 213-217.

Müller, F.M. (1879): *Origine et développement de la religion, étudiés à la lumière des religions de l'Inde*. (Transl. of Lectures on the Origin and Growth of Religion, as illustrated by the Religions of India, Hibbert Lectures, 1878.) Paris: C. Reinwald.

Muṇḍaka Upaniṣad = Limaye and Vadekar, 1958: 38-47.

Mus, Paul (1935): *Barabuḍur. Esquisse d'une histoire du bouddhisme fondée sur la critique archéologique des textes*. 2 vols. Hanoi.

Nakamura, Hajime (1983): *A History of Early Vedānta Philosophy*. Part One. Translated into English by Trevor Leggett e.a. Delhi: Motilal Banarsidass. (Religions of Asia Series, 1.)

Nyāyabhāṣya. ŚrīmadVātsyāyanamunikṛtabhāṣyaŚrīViśvanāthabhaṭṭācārya-kṛtavṛttisametāni Śrī-Gautamamunipraṇīta-Nyāyasūtrāṇi. Ed. by Nāgeśa Digambara Śāstrī Jośī. Poona: Ānandāśrama. 1922.

O'Flaherty, Wendy Doniger (1973): *Śiva, the Erotic Ascetic*. Oxford University Press paperback, 1981.

[106] O'Flaherty, Wendy Doniger (1980): *Women, Androgynes, and Other Mythological Beasts*. Chicago and London: University of Chicago Press.

Oldenberg, Hermann (1917): *Die Religion des Veda*. Zweite Auflage. Reprint: Magnus-Verlag, Stuttgart.

Olivelle, Patrick (1974): "The notion of āśrama in the Dharmasūtras." *Wiener Zeitschrift für die Kunde Südasiens* 18, 27-35.

Olivelle, Patrick (1974a): *The Origin and the Early Development of Buddhist Monachism*. Colombo: Gunasena.

Olivelle, Patrick (1981): "Contributions to the semantic history of saṃnyāsa." *Journal of the American Oriental Society* 101, 265-274.

Olivelle, Patrick (1984): "Renouncer and renunciation in the Dharmaśāstras." In: *Studies in Dharmaśāstra*, ed. by Richard W. Lariviere. Calcutta: Firma KLM. Pp. 81-152.

Olivelle, Patrick (1992): *Saṃnyāsa Upaniṣads. Hindu scriptures on asceticism and renunciation*. Translated with introduction and notes. Oxford University Press.

Olivelle, Patrick (1993): *The Āśrama System. The history and hermeneutics of a religious institution*. Oxford University Press.

Olivelle, Patrick (1995): *Rules and Regulations of Brahmanical Asceticism. Yatidharmasamuccaya of Yādava Prakāśa*. Edited and translated. State University of New York Press.

Padoux, André (1987): "Contributions à l'étude du mantraśāstra, III: Le japa." *Bulletin de l'Ecole Française d'Extrême-Orient* 76, 117-159.

Pande, Govind Chandra (1974): *Studies in the Origins of Buddhism*. Third edition. Delhi: Motilal Banarsidass. 1983.

Paramahaṃsaparivrājaka Upaniṣad = Schrader, 1912: 277-89.

Patañjali: *Vyākaraṇa-Mahābhāṣya*. 3 vols. Edited by F. Kielhorn. Third Edition by K.V. Abhyankar. Poona: Bhandarkar Oriental Research Institute. 1962-72.

Praśastapāda: *Padārthadharmasaṅgraha. The Praśastapāda Bhāshya with Commentary Nyāyakandali of Sridhara*, edited by Vindhyesvari Prasad Dvivedin. Reprint. Delhi: Sri Satguru. 1984.

Rhys Davids, T.W. (tr.)(1899): *Dialogues of the Buddha*. Part I. London: The Pali Text Society. Reprint 1977.

Rhys Davids, T.W. and C.A.F. (tr.)(1921): *Dialogues of the Buddha*. Part III. [107]
London: The Pali Text Society. Reprint 1977.

Śābara Bhāṣya. Edited by Kāśīnātha Vāsudevaśāstrī Abhyaṃkara and Gaṇeśaśāstrī Jośī. Poona: Ānandāśrama.

Scharfe, Hartmut (1987): "Nomadisches Erbgut in der indischen Tradition." *Hinduismus und Buddhismus. Festschrift für Ulrich Schneider*. Ed. Harry Falk. Freiburg: Hedwig Falk. Pp. 300-308.

Scheuer, Jacques (1975): "Śiva dans le Mahābhārata: l'histoire d'Ambā / Śikhaṇīin." *Puruṣārtha* 2, 67-86.

Schmidt, Hanns-Peter (1968): "The origin of ahiṃsā." *Mélanges d'Indianisme à la Mémoire de Louis Renou*. Paris: E. de Boccard. (Publications de l'Institut de Civilisation Indienne, 28.) Pp. 625-655.

Schneider, Ulrich (1989): *Einführung in den Hinduismus*. Darmstadt: Wissenschaftliche Buchgesellschaft.

Schrader, F. Otto (1910): "Zum Ursprung der Lehre vom Saṃsāra." *Zeitschrift der Deutschen Morgenländischen Gesellschaft* 64, 333-335. Reprint: *Kleine Schriften* (Wiesbaden, 1983) pp. 148-150.

Schrader, F. Otto (ed.)(1912): *The Minor Upaniṣads*. Vol. I: Saṃnyāsa-Upaniṣads. Madras: Adyar Library.

Schwanbeck, E.A. (1846): *Megasthenis Indica*. Bonn. (Reprint: Amsterdam 1966.)

Shee, Monika (1986): *Tapas und tapasvin in den erzählenden Partien des Mahābhārata*. Reinbek: Inge Wezler. (Studien zur Indologie und Iranistik, Dissertationen Band 1.)

Siegel, Lee (1991): *Net of Magic. Wonders and deceptions in India*. University of Chicago Press.

Silburn, Lilian (1955): *Instant et cause. Le discontinu dans la pensée philosophique de l'Inde*. Paris: J. Vrin.

Skurzak, Ludwik (1948): *Études sur l'origine de l'ascétisme indien*. Wroclaw. (Travaux de la Société des Sciences et des Lettres de Wroclaw. Seria A, Nr. 15.)

[108] Sprockhoff, Joachim Friedrich (1976): *Saṃnyāsa. Quellenstudien zur Askese im Hinduismus*, I. Untersuchungen über die Saṃnyāsa-Upaniṣads. Wiesbaden: Franz Steiner. (Abhandlungen für die Kunde des Morgenlandes, Band XLII, 1.)

Sprockhoff, Joachim Friedrich (1979): "Die Alten im alten Indien: ein Versuch nach brahmanischen Quellen." *Saeculum* 30, 374-433.

Sprockhoff, Joachim Friedrich (1980): "Die feindlichen Toten und der befriedende Tote." In: *Leben und Tod in den Religionen: Symbol und Wirklichkeit*. Hrsg. Gunther Stephenson. Darmstadt: Wissenschaftliche Buchgesellschaft. Pp. 263-284.

Sprockhoff, Joachim Friedrich (1981): "Āraṇyaka und Vānaprastha in der vedischen Literatur." *Wiener Zeitschrift für die Kunde Südasiens* 25, 19-90.

Sprockhoff, Joachim Friedrich (1984): "Āraṇyaka und Vānaprastha in der vedischen Literatur." *Wiener Zeitschrift für die Kunde Südasiens* 28, 5-43.

Sprockhoff, Joachim Friedrich (1987): "Kaṭhaśruti und Mānavaśrautasūtra: eine Nachlese zur Resignation." *Studien zur Indologie und Iranistik* 13/14, 235-257.

Sprockhoff, Joachim Friedrich (1989): "Versuch einer deutschen Übersetzung der Kaṭhaśruti und der Kaṭharudra-Upaniṣad." *Asiatische Studien / Études Asiatiques* 43, 137-163.

Sprockhoff, Joachim Friedrich (1991): "Laghu-Saṃnyāsa-Upaniṣad und Kuṇḍikā-Upaniṣad: Versuch einer deutschen Übersetzung." *Études Asiatiques / Asiatische Studien* 45, 107-131.

Sprockhoff, Joachim Friedrich (1991a): "Āraṇyaka und Vānaprastha in der vedischen Literatur." *Wiener Zeitschrift für die Kunde Südasiens* 35, 5-46.

Srinivasan, Doris (1984): "Unhinging Śiva from the Indus civilization." *Journal of the Royal Asiatic Society* (1984), 77-89.

[109] Staal, Frits (1983): *Agni. The vedic ritual of the fire altar*. Vol. I. Berkeley: Asian Humanities Press.

Stutley, Margaret and James (1986): *A Dictionary of Hinduism*. Its Mythology, Folklore and Development 1500 B.C.-A.D. 1500. New Delhi: Heritage Publishers.

Sullivan, Bruce M. (1990): *Kṛṣṇa Dvaipāyana Vyāsa and the Mahābhārata: a new interpretation*. Leiden: E.J. Brill.

Sūyagaḍaṃgasutta. Ed. Muni Jambūvijaya. Jaina-Āgama-Series No. 2 (2). Bombay: Shrī Mahāvīra Jaina Vidyālaya. 1978.

Śvetāśvatara Upaniṣad = Limaye and Vadekar, 1958: 283-300.

Takakusu, J. (1904): "La Sāṃkhyakārikā." *Bulletin de l'École Française d'Extrême-Orient* 4, 1-65 & 978-1064.

Ṭhāṇaṃgasutta. In: *Ṭhāṇaṃgasuttaṃ and Samavāyāṃgasuttaṃ*, ed. Muni Jambūvijaya. Jaina-Āgama-Series No. 3. Bombay: Shrī Mahāvīra Jaina Vidyālaya. 1985. Pp. 1-322.

Thibaut, George (tr.)(1904): *Vedānta-Sūtras*. 3 parts. Reprint: Motilal Banarsidass, Delhi, 1971-1973. (Sacred Books of the East 34, 38, 48.)

Thieme, Paul (1963): "Agastya und Lopāmudrā." *Zeitschrift der Deutschen Morgenländischen Gesellschaft* 113, 69-79. Reprint: *Kleine Schriften* (Wiesbaden, 1984) pp. 202-212.

Thite, Ganesh Umakant (1975): *Sacrifice in the Brāhmaṇa-Texts*. Poona: University of Poona.

Thomas, Edward J. (1933): *The History of Buddhist Thought*. London: Routledge & Kegan Paul. 1971.

Tsuchida, Ryutaro (1996): "Versuch einer Interpretation von Chāndogya-Upaniṣad 2,23." *Studien zur Indologie und Iranistik* 20 (Festschrift Paul Thieme), 453-484.

Tsuchida, Ryutaro (1996a): "An interpretation of Baudhāyana-dharma-sūtra 2, 11, 26." *Tōyō Bunka Kenkyū Shokiyō* 130, 181-211.

Tsuchidą, Ryutaro (1997): "Die Weltentsagung der Ikṣvāku-Könige." *Memoirs of the Institute of Oriental Culture* (University of Tokyo) 133, 105-161.

Tull, Herman W. (1989): *The Vedic Origins of Karma. Cosmos as man in ancient Indian myth and ritual*. Albany: State University of New York Press. (SUNY Series in Hindu Studies.)

Vaikhānasa Dharma Sūtra. In: *Vaikhānasasmārtasūtram*, edited by W. Caland. Calcutta: Asiatic Society of Bengal. 1927.

van Buitenen, J.A.B. (tr.)(1973, 1975, 1978): *The Mahābhārata*. 3 volumes, covering 5 books, have appeared. The University of Chicago Press

[110] Varenne, Jean (1960): *La Mahā Nārāyaṇa Upaniṣad*. Édition critique, avec une traduction française, une étude, des notes et, en annexe, la Prāṇāgnihotra Upaniṣad. Publications de l'Institut de Civilisation Indienne, 11 et 13. Paris: E. de Boccard. 2 vol.

Varenne, Jean (tr.)(1971): *Upanishads du Yoga*. Gallimard/Unesco.

Vasiṣṭha Dharma Sūtra. The Vāsiṣṭhadharmaśāstram, edited by Alois Anton Führer. Poona: B.O.R.I. Institute. 1930. (Bombay Sanskrit and Prakrit Series, 23.)

Viyāhapaṇṇattisutta. Edited by Pt. Bechardas J. Doshi (for part II assisted by Pt. Amritlal Mohanlal Bhojak). Bombay: Shrī Mahāvīra Jaina Vidyālaya. 1974-78. 2 parts. (Jaina-Āgama-Series No. 4.)

Warder, A.K. (1980): *Indian Buddhism*. Second revised edition. Delhi: Motilal Banarsidass.

Wezler, Albrecht (1978): *Die waren 'Speiseresteesser' (Skt. vighasāśin)*. Wiesbaden: Franz Steiner. (Akademie der Wissenschaften und der Literatur, Abhandlungen der geistes- und sozialwissenschaftlichen Klasse, Jahrgang 1978 Nr. 5.)

Wezler, Albrecht (1979): "Śamīka und Śṛṅgin. Zum Verständnis einer askesekritischen Erzählung aus dem Mahābhārata." *Wiener Zeitschrift für die Kunde Südasiens* 23, 29-62.

Wiltshire, Martin G. (1990): *Ascetic Figures before and in Early Buddhism*. The emergence of Gautama as the Buddha. Berlin – New York: Mouton de Gruyter. (Religion and Reason, 30.)

Winternitz, Moriz (1908): *Geschichte der indischen Literatur*. Band 1: Einleitung, der Veda, die volkstümlichen Epen und die Purāṇas. Stuttgart: K.F. Koehler. 1968.

Winternitz, Moriz (1926): "Zur Lehre von den Āśramas." *Beiträge zur Literaturwissenschaft und Geistesgeschichte Indiens*. Festgabe Hermann Jacobi zum 75. Geburtstag. Hrsg. v. Willibald Kirfel. Bonn: Fritz Klopp. Pp. 215-227.

[111] Witzel, Michael (1984): "The earliest form of the idea of rebirth in India." *Proceedings of the Thirty-First International Congress of Human Sciences in Asia and North Africa* (Tōkyō-Kyōto, 31st August – 7th September 1983). Edited by Yamamoto Tatsurō. Vol. I. Tōkyō: The Tōhō Gakkai (The Institute of Eastern Culture). Pp. 145-146.

Wolz-Gottwald, Eckard (1990): "Zur Bedeutung des Asketentums für die Entstehung des Āyurveda." *Journal of the European Āyurvedic Society* 1, 125-126.

Woodward, F.L. (tr.)(1927): *The Book of the Kindred Sayings* (Saṃyutta-Nikāya). Part IV. London: Pali Text Society. Reprint 1972.

Yuktidīpikā. Edited by Ram Chandra Pandeya. Delhi: Motilal Banarsidass. 1967.

Zimmer, Heinrich (1879): *Altindisches Leben. Die Cultur der vedischen Arier nach den Saṃhitā dargestellt.* Nachdruck: Georg Olms, Hildesheim – New York. 1973.

Zysk, Kenneth G. (1990): "The Indian ascetic traditions and the origins of āyurvedic medicine." *Journal of the European Āyurvedic Society* 1, 119-124.

Zysk, Kenneth G. (1991): *Asceticism and Healing in Ancient India*. Medicine in the Buddhist Monastery. Delhi: Oxford University Press.

Abbreviations

AB *Aitareya Brāhmaṇa*
AhS *Ahirbudhnya Saṃhitā*
AN *Aṅguttara Nikāya* (PTS edition)
ĀpDhS *Āpastamba Dharmasūtra*, ed. Bühler
AV *Atharva Veda*
BAU *Bṛhadāraṇyaka Upaniṣad*
BDhS *Baudhāyana Dharma Sūtra*
ChU *Chāndogya Upaniṣad*
CPS *Catuṣpariṣat Sūtra*
DN *Dīgha Nikāya* (PTS edition)
GDhS *Gautama Dharma Sūtra*
Jā *Jātaka* (= Fausbøll, 1877-1896)
KU *Kaṭha Upaniṣad*
MBh *Mahābhārata* (crit. ed.)
MN *Majjhima Nikāya* (PTS edition)
MŚS *Mānava Śrauta Sūtra*
PTS Pali Text Society
Pupph *Pupphiyāo* (= Deleu, 1966: 117-124)
ŚB *Śatapatha Brāhmaṇa, Mādhyandina version*
SN *Saṃyutta Nikāya* (PTS edition)
Sn *Suttanipāta* (PTS edition)
ŚŚS *Śāṅkhāyana Śrauta Sūtra*
Sūy *Sūyagaḍaṃgasutta*
ŚvetUp *Śvetāśvatara Upaniṣad* [113]
T. Taishō ed. of Buddhist Tripiṭaka in Chinese
Ṭhāṇ *Ṭhāṇaṃgasutta*
Uvav *Uvavāiya* (see Leumann, 1883)
VasDhS *Vasiṣṭha Dharma Sūtra*
VDhS *Vaikhānasa Dharma Sūtra*
Vin *Vinaya* (PTS edition)
Viy *Viyāhapaṇṇattisutta*